THE SIX-CRYSTAL

by
STEPHANIE CLAUS

Deep
Pacific
Press

THE SIX-CRYSTAL

The Quest of Remembering our Soul's Calling and Mission on Earth

Copyright © 2023 Stephanie Claus

Deep Pacific Press

Deep Pacific Press
117 E 37th Street #580
Loveland, CO 80538
www.DeepPacificPress.com

All rights reserved. No part of this publication may be reproduced, distributed, or transmitted in any form or by any means, including photocopying, recording, or other electronic or mechanical methods, without the prior written permission of the publisher, except in the case of brief quotations embodied in critical reviews and certain other non-commercial uses permitted by copyright law. For permission requests, write to the publisher, addressed "Attention: Permissions Coordinator," at the address above.

Front cover image by Charlie Orellana
Cover design by Patrick Knowles
Back cover photo by Landa Penders

ISBN 978-1-956108-15-6 (paperback)
ISBN 978-1-956108-16-3 (eBook)

Email: connect@stephanieclaus.com

www.stephanieclaus.com
www.thesixcrystal.com

Written to my younger self,
who at times felt very different in this world.

I dedicate this book to the 'crazy ones'
who carry the future within.

And I send out a signal to my soul tribe:

We are One.

With Love and Devotion,

Stephanie

*What happens when you find out
there is a much greater purpose to your life?*

BEFORE YOU DIVE IN ...

Nothing but Magic.
That is how I have experienced the writing of this book.

A portal into Remembrance.
That is what I believe this book truly is.

Just a fantasy novel — or closer to reality than you might think?
I'll leave it up to you to find your own answer to this question.

✱

This book is written for anyone who wants to know themselves more deeply, live their purpose, and align their life to their soul's mission.

This is for those of you who feel called to a different way of being and living, and who want to co-create a thriving future for humanity and life on Earth.

✱

When I said 'yes' to writing a book, I didn't realise what I was getting myself into. This book has become like a dear companion — yes, I truly see and experience it as a Multidimensional Being with its own consciousness — and I have come to trust its guidance.

And now it has found its way into your hands (or in front of your eyes if you have a digital version). I'm guessing that may be the consequence of what seems like coincidence, or a series of synchronistic events.

This is not a traditional fiction book. Nor is this just a fantasy book. It exists outside of any category. The best way to describe this book is to call it a spiritual initiation — an activation key — an encoded manuscript that evokes healing, transformation and awakening.

That's why I would love to share a few suggestions before you dive into the story, so you can have the best possible reading experience.

How to Read This Book

✶ READ WITH YOUR HEART, NOT YOUR MIND

The mind, grasping for logic and sense, cannot understand the multidimensional nature of our reality. You are invited to receive this book as a transmission that speaks to your heart and soul.

✶ LET THE STORY BE A MIRROR

This book may touch upon your own life themes and be a trigger to reveal both your purpose and greatness, as well as your shadows and wounds. I invite you to let the stories resonate with your own journey and unveil what may have been hidden from your conscious eye.

✶ EXPLORE THE MEANING OF THE KEY CODES

Each chapter ends with a 'key code' that you can see as a ZIP file that holds much more information. You are invited to tune in or meditate with these key codes and see what insights and knowledge they want to reveal to you personally.

✶ FIND THE ANSWERS YOU ARE SEEKING

If, at any point, the book leaves you with questions unanswered (especially by the end of the book), then tune into your heart or higher self and ask what you want to know. You are invited to imagine yourself as a co-creator of this book, able to see beyond what has been written, so trust your own seeing and imagination.

✶ WELCOME TO PLAY

You can use this book as an 'inner work-book'. After you've read the book once, you can make it your companion — for example, open the book at a random page to see what theme or message wants to be highlighted for you that day.

You are invited to play with this book in your own unique way. Or you can join a 'Book Quest' and explore the topics in this book together with other readers (more details can be found at the back of this book).

When you finish this book, it's up to you to write your own sequel in the form of your own life's journey. That's how we each allow this book to become even more alive.

May you receive this book as the activation portal it is intended to be.

Enjoy reading!

With Soul,
Stephanie Claus

TABLE OF CONTENTS

Before You Dive In … .... *i*
How to Read This Book .... *iii*
Prologue: The Six-Crystal Speaks *1*
1. A Preview of Coming Attractions *5*
2. Crashing Down *7*
3. Egypt Calls *11*
4. #starseeds *13*
5. Waking Up Anew *15*
6. Amnesia?! *19*
7. Chicken Wings *22*
8. Scars from a Past Life *27*
9. Reclamation *32*
10. Angelic Presence *34*
11. Inside the King's Chamber *36*
12. Time Travel Box *40*
13. Meeting Beyond the Veil *47*
14. Doctor! Doctor! *52*
15. Time to Move On *54*
16. The Witch Hunt *55*
17. Finding Her Tone *59*
18. New Eyes to See *61*
19. A Spark of Light *64*
20. Calling Out *68*
21. Like a House of Cards *72*
22. The Design *77*
23. Just a Crazy Dream? *81*
24. Australia Calls *83*
25. Contact *85*
26. What is Oneness?! *87*
27. The Six-Crystal Activation *89*
28. The TOO MUCH Girl *93*
29. Toughen up, Boy! *97*
30. The Memory of Divine Union *101*
31. Homeache *104*
32. Home is Here *108*
33. The Underwater Temple *109*
34. Meeting Yu-Ka-Na *116*

35. From Crazy to Genius	119
36. Light Language Activation	124
37. Communication Line	128
38. Simultaneity	130
39. Divine Orchestration	132
40. SiX Sees All	137
41. White Butterflies	138
42. Inner Union	142
43. Coming Home	144
44. Putting the Pieces Together	146
45. The Triad is Born	150
46. Like an Open Book	153
47. When Scarcity Kicks In	156
48. And Much, Much More	161
49. A Walk on the Beach	166
50. Channel SiX	168
51. Unravelling Oneness	171
52. The Redwoods	177
53. Pure Intent	182
54. Wake-Up Call	188
55. Falling Apart	190
56. Waterfalls	195
57. Heaven on Earth	199
58. Upgrading the Six-Crystal Activation	202
59. One Mission — One Team	206
60. Just Like a Dream	211
61. Newsflash	213
62. Love from Venus	215
63. Meeting Up with Yu-Ka-Na	218
64. At the Park	222
65. Catching Up	225
66. The Highest Potential	227
The Six-Crystal Speaks	241
Blurred Lines	245
My Invitation to You	253
Possible Next Steps	255
Recommended Resources	257
Gratitude	261

PROLOGUE: THE SIX-CRYSTAL SPEAKS

Robbie dropped his pen. Staring at the words in his journal, he wondered if he had just written the beginning of a sci-fi novel. In truth, his life's mission had just been delivered to his doorstep.

About to close his journal, he decided he just had to read it once more. With a deep breath in, Robbie glanced at his notes as if they contained a secret code.

I AM THE SIX-CRYSTAL

An impeccable, multidimensional design with six points
spinning in complete harmony, tethered in a unique constellation,
exploring different pathways towards the same goal.
Everything that is birthed from this design
has the Six-Crystal embedded at its core.

We appear as a collective consciousness.
And so, the *I Am* equals the *We Are*.
As the Six-Crystal, *We are One* and *Move as One*.

It is our desire to experience our Oneness
in all forms and all ways.

This is the design.
This is the desire.
This is the intention.

With a big sigh, Robbie closed his journal. He had never heard of anything like the Six-Crystal before. So, now what?

His first attempt at channelling information from his higher self through writing certainly was not like the classic 'what is my next step?' conversation, nor the typical Q&A he had seen in other channellings with Abraham Hicks or Bashar. He had no idea where his channelling came from, and yet his inner Knowing whispered, *"This is real."*

1. A PREVIEW OF COMING ATTRACTIONS

And so, she Remembered.

Ana stared at the ocean. Her feet in the sand, the wind blowing through her long, curly red hair and the sound of a helicopter whirring by. Nothing could disturb her as her gaze turned inward.

She Remembered the Six-Crystal within her heart. She knew she was both one with it, and a part of it — the creator and receiver of it. Tears of recognition welled up in her eyes.

Ana was standing on the beach, yet simultaneously, she was activating the Six-Crystal within her awareness, as if she were starting up the engines of a rocket ship. The astral geometric form began to spin in her heart, expanding with every breath she took.

She understood that sooner or later, her realisation had to be reflected in her outside world. As within, so without. As above, so below. That's universal law. Knowing she was destined to experience the Six-Crystal here on Earth, in human form, Ana squealed with the excitement of anticipation.

"It's just by design. It is my destiny," she whispered.

She thought of Robbie, while deep gratitude filled her heart as she looked back on how they first met, just two seemingly ordinary teenagers who drank their stress away and had no clue there was a greater purpose to their lives. Both had been veiled by forgetfulness.

Now they were both waking up — not just to who they were

beyond their human meat suits, as a soul on a journey, but to a greater divine design that marked the greater interconnectedness of us all and seemed to weave different time-space dimensions into one pattern. Her mind couldn't grasp any of it. Luckily, she had stopped putting her mind in the driver's seat of her life on the day of the accident, and instead started listening to her heart and intuition.

And so, she Remembered. She *Remembered!*

To a spectator, she was just standing at the coastline. To Ana, it felt like a timeless moment. And yet, it was this very moment that catalysed Ana into a whole new chapter of her life. Little did she know what was to come.

Her mind could only glimpse the potentials of the future, yet her heart knew and invited her to open up to a new reality, and most importantly, a new way of operating.

From One into We.

Life as an independent, separate human would soon be over. On one hand, she would become more of Her-Self, her Essence, while simultaneously die to all she had been, shedding the roles, expectations and limiting beliefs she had taken on through her upbringing. On the other hand, she would open up to a more united and collective way of living.

She had forgotten her true nature, but now ... she Remembered.

KEY CODE: REMEMBRANCE

2. CRASHING DOWN

A white butterfly.

That's the last thing that passed before Ana's eyes right before she passed out.

"*This doesn't make sense,*" was her last thought as the blackness came. And then ... nothing.

9 hours earlier ...

Robbie and Ana loved going out. Like many millennials, they liked to hang out at the park after a busy work week, kicking off the weekend with Budweiser beers and a portable speaker blasting their favourite music. They didn't care if they disturbed the passers-by who strolled by for a quiet walk. 'Friday Night at the Park' had become the place to be for everyone in Redding between the ages of eighteen and thirty.

After sunset, they would go out to eat pizza and find a bar where they could dance. At least, Ana would dance. You'd better not think about interrupting her Friday night dance routine, as that's where she let loose, engaging her fiery spirit and shaking off all the worries and stress she'd built up during the week. Her dance night was her church.

It seemed like just another typical Friday night. Robert — called "Robbie" by his friends — was getting wasted at the bar, while Ana shook her booty to the latest hit of Dua Lipa. Ana wasn't into beer, but after every few songs she'd go to Robbie to get another shot of tequila. She loved the feeling of getting tipsy in her head while her body was moving. She would forget about the world and lose herself in the rhythm. This was where she wanted to be forever …

Robbie grabbed her by the arm.

"What the hell are you doing?!"

"Time to go. Come on!" he yelled above the loud music.

"No!" she pulled her arm back as she turned away and continued dancing.

Robbie pulled her close again and barked into her ear, "I am going NOW! If you wanna act stupid and stay, fine, but I'm out of here!"

"What the fuck?!" Ana replied in disbelief.

Ana wasn't done dancing, but neither did she like to hang out there alone. She secretly saw Robbie as her private bodyguard, making sure she didn't get unwanted attention or the typical slap on the butt from some drunk guy. Afraid she would end up in a ditch if she tried to get back up the hill by herself in the middle of the night, she followed him outside.

"Robbie! What's up, dude? Why are we leaving? I'm not done dancing!"

"Well, I am done. It's 3:00 a.m. Come on," Robbie said, determined.

He jiggled his keys, struggling to find the right one. He'd gotten a little too self-assured as he had sipped one too many beers and now felt a little dizzy, but neither cared, as they were used to driving with alcohol under their belt. After all, they lived in a small town, and no one really cared. It was just what you did on a Friday night. Can't call Mommy to pick you up when you're twenty-five, can you?

The music blasted out loud. He would only play System of a Down when he didn't want to talk. Ana was still upset. And drunk.

"I hate it, Robbie. I hate that you're this selfish dick who just decides for his boo that she is done dancing. Like, what am I — your puppet or something? I am done with this! I'm going to get my own car soon, and then, Robbie …"

"And then what, Ana? Then what? You wanna go off dancing? You wanna go out on your own?" Pissed off, he pulled the car over and stopped as he showed her the door. "Then GO! You're a free woman! You can do and go wherever you want to. I ain't got a say in your whereabouts, Miss Ana Bell!"

"Oh, shut up and just drive me home, for God's sake." She turned her head away and stared out her window into the dark night. It was rare for their Friday night to end up this heated, except for those nights that ended with some steamy sex in the back seat of his car.

Infuriated, Robbie accelerated his Chevy Camaro as if it were a Ferrari, climbing the mountain hill at full speed to drop Ana off at her mother's house. He loved his independence and had been putting off living together.

"What are you doing, Robbie?!" Ana asked as he reached over to the passenger's seat, looking for God-knows-what, while tilting the steering wheel.

"Robbie, watch out!" Ana shrieked as the car veered towards the mountain.

Caught off guard, Robbie quickly pulled his steering wheel in the other direction. Seconds too late, he hit the brakes. Ana screamed as the car burst through the guardrail at 60 MPH, hurling them into the pitch-black abyss.

The car crashed into the ditch at the bottom of the hill in just moments, leaving no time for her life to pass before her eyes. And yet, it felt as if she was in a still point in time, where every second felt like an eternity, and everything played out in slow motion.

In disbelief, Ana observed herself, Robbie and the car flying downwards at the uttermost slowest pace. She heard her own scream leave her mouth as her body realised what was happening and survival mode kicked in.

Out of the blue, a white butterfly passed in front of the windshield. A frown crinkled her forehead, then the thought, *"This doesn't make sense,"* right before the blackness hit.

KEY CODE: CATALYST

3. EGYPT CALLS

Tiny had never seen stars so bright. She could even see the thick band of the Milky Way with its dark, galactic centre. The vastness and lucidity of the night sky almost made her feel like she could reach out her hand and touch the stars, but her mind knew better. The cool sand reminded her that she still had her feet on the ground. The silence that night was almost palpable as there wasn't even a breeze.

It had been quite the ride to get there, leaving everything she knew behind to end up in no man's land, in the Sinai Desert of all places on Earth, to … find herself?

∗

Tiny, pronounced 'T-in-ee,' grew up in a tiny village in Taiwan as the youngest of her family. As the only girl, she easily became the object of teasing for her three older brothers. Her slender posture and short stature gave rise to mocking her first name. She had a short black bob with bangs and her Asian features would reveal her origin if she was out in the world, yet at home she easily disappeared in the crowd and felt like a nobody.

Tiny had an introverted nature. She often felt shy and insecure, especially when being asked a question she didn't know the answer to. Her aim was to not upset people and keep everyone at peace.

Nonetheless, by the time she turned twenty she could no longer ignore a pull from within. She'd had enough of life in Chenggong, the traditional fisherman's village she had lived in since birth. Fun fact:

Tiny had watched Disney movies like *Moana* and *The Croods*, movies that evoked her desire within to sail out across the sea, to find her tribe — whatever that meant — and answer the call for adventure.

Life seemed so small in Chenggong. She had a sense there was more — more to her, more to life, and more to how life could be and what was meant for her. She was seeking something she couldn't pinpoint, which caused her many restless nights.

And yet, the call from within had pulled her out of her comfort cave in Taiwan and made her set sail for Egypt when she had just turned twenty-one. What happened there would be a story for the books.

KEY CODE: SOUL'S CALLING

4. #STARSEEDS

A tear rolled down Tiny's cheek as she looked up to the night sky. She felt such a pull towards the stars, or was it from the stars? She couldn't tell the difference, but somehow, she was dreaming of going back there.

"*Going back?*" What was that about? She couldn't explain this sadness, this indefinable heartache.

She remembered that before she left Taiwan, she had come across the tag #starseeds on Instagram. A whole new world had opened up to her, yes, the one she had been longing for. She didn't even realise how alone she had felt her whole life until she started seeing all these 'Light Beings' share their unique experiences. Gosh, how grateful she felt that she had access to the Internet. There were times when opening social media spiked her insecurity, as she didn't have big boobs, no lip fillers and didn't do a workout to lift her butt. She couldn't even relate to that way of chasing fake beauty. But discovering these 'Light Beings' online lifted her spirit, so she only followed accounts from people with tags like #spiritualseeker, #lightworker, #cosmicbeing, #lightbeing, and of course, #starseeds.

Tiny had read about starseeds having 'homesickness' for their home in the stars. It seemed otherworldly, yet somehow it matched her own experience. She had just never had a name for it and hadn't realised she wasn't the only one feeling that way.

She recognized all the 'typical starseed characteristics' she found online:

* A feeling like she doesn't belong here, as if Earth is a foreign place.
* Feeling different. She didn't feel like she fitted into the world.
* An unexplainable connection to the stars, even having a sense of having a home beyond this world.
* Small talk feels like a waste of time. She always wants to get beyond the surface.
* Having a sense of purpose and feeling like she is here for a reason.
* Having a remembrance of being more than just the mind and body.
* Understanding that this life is part of a greater soul's journey.
* A wisdom seeker, looking for the deeper meaning of life.
* Intuitive and empathic. A highly sensitive person.
* Able to easily read between the lines and pick up on nuances, reading people's energy instead of just listening to their words, which sometimes feels like a different language.

A wave of relief washed over her as she felt understood in a way she had never been before. Tiny didn't feel like she could share this with her family or friends, as they would think she was crazy, but apparently, there were more people like her, literally, all over the world. Maybe this was her tribe?

KEY CODE: STARSEED

5. WAKING UP ANEW

Ana got lucky. She had survived the car crash with only a few bruises and contusions, as if a guardian angel had protected her. She had blacked out for a few hours, but later woke up in the hospital.

Robbie had not been so lucky and was still in a coma. A few weeks passed by without any change. His organs and body were operational, but he hadn't yet given any signs of being conscious. Ana visited him every day and read from what would become his favourite poetry book, *Rumi's Little Book of Life*. Every day, she hoped for evidence of him coming back to life.

The car crash had not left her with many scars, but it did create a ripple in her life. The doctors had warned her to watch out for PTSD symptoms, but whatever they said went in one ear and out the other. Ana, as per usual, had her own way of dealing with things.

She didn't need to have a full-on near-death experience to realise she couldn't continue to waste her life, as she and Robbie had been gambling with their lives, blinded by a mix of innocence and ignorance.

The accident shook Ana awake, and made her make some extreme decisions, thanks to her dramatic nature. She unfriended everyone on Facebook and Instagram who reminded her of her 'old life' and deleted their numbers in her phone. She ghosted all her friends at Redding and told her mother she had to move out, find her own apartment and deal with life and her 'shit' herself. She wanted to be alone. Even Friday nights at the park were now nothing but a distraction.

Before the accident, Ana had been thrilled to be part of a female-owned business where she could finish up her two-year on-the-job training as an interior designer, but now the thought of going back to remodelling houses made her feel dull. She simply couldn't bring herself to go back to what she had been doing, so she applied for at least a month of medical leave.

Moving an hour further north, Ana found a cabin for rent in the middle of the woods with a magical view of Mount Shasta through the back window. Her new home marked a new beginning, and with that came new routines. Every day she woke up at 6:00 a.m. and prayed for one hour, something she hadn't done since she was a kid, but she felt *if not now, then when?* She prayed for Robbie to wake up, she prayed for Peace, and prayed for Healing for all who needed it on Earth. She prayed for her life to change, to figure out what to do next and find out: "who am I, really?"

Her prayer soon turned into a daily yoga practice, and later was also followed by meditation. Ana wanted to calm her monkey mind and experience the stillness she had felt at the time of the car crash. Ironically, in that moment when death felt so close, she also experienced the greatest serenity, a sense of peace and stillness that was unparalleled.

With every day, Ana's desire to reach this stillness became stronger. She wanted to become the witness and to be aware as life played out in front of her eyes, to be Zen, to be like Buddha, to quiet the mind and be one with life.

Ana had always had a busy and fiery spirit, but as she now sat daily on her meditation pillow, she was starting to look more and more like a real yogi. A calmness would descend upon her and the inner restlessness she had always known would fade away. It was still challenging, but with practice, she was able to remain in her own centre more often and stay in the eye of the storm, no matter what happened around her. Sometimes, she wondered if she had become immune to life, a little numb, or if what she felt was true peace. She couldn't tell the difference, but knew the challenge was to take that peace with her from the meditation pillow and into her daily life.

She was no longer the Ana her friends and family had known and had become a different version of herself. Looking back, she saw how fucked-up her life had been. Not because she had a terrible life, but because of the fucked-up way people were living. What was actually real in this world? It seemed like everyone around her was more like a puppet on a string, dancing to the tune of others.

Mothers would give up their own dreams in the name of love for their children. Children would do everything they could to get some love and attention from their parents. Peer pressure made teenagers do the craziest things, like soaking a tampon in vodka, say what?! Girls would dress up, or barely dress, to impress a boy, not because they felt sexy, but because their black eyeliner and highlighter would hide their insecurity, just like the latest filter on Instagram. Looking at the world, she saw just one great show of shadows, and realised how the car crash had been a catalyst for her to step out of that show.

"Still a drama queen, but no more fake shows. No, thank you!" she declared out loud.

Ana exchanged bingeing Netflix for reading books about spiritual awakening, mindfulness and self-healing. She also turned to a mostly organic, plant-based diet and continued her yoga and meditation practice at home. She felt more peaceful, while simultaneously couldn't bear the ache Robbie's coma was causing to her heart. It was hard to believe six months had already passed and he was still in … she couldn't even think of the word without her eyes welling up with tears.

KEY CODE: TURNING POINT

6. AMNESIA?!

Ana had only just turned nineteen when she sought the help of a gynaecologist.

"Miss Bell, come on in."

Ana entered the gynaecologist's office. His military posture and emotionless face always gave her shivers. A month earlier, she had been there for an examination as she had been suffering unbearable period pain, and recently, even had intense aches when Robbie penetrated her. So young and inexperienced, she had felt extremely uncomfortable being touched by the doctor.

"Well, Miss Bell, the good news is you don't have any STIs, but the bad news is," he paused for a moment, "I believe we have found some scar tissue in the vagina. Most of it seems healed, however, it might become sensitive during penetration or during menstruation when the uterus is shedding. It is very unlikely you would have not been aware of this before, as these scars look like the remains of sharp cuts in your vagina, which would have caused excruciating pain at the time they occurred. So, I have to ask you — do you want to report any abuse?" the old, grey-haired doctor inquired, maintaining his poker face.

Ana's mouth fell wide open. She stammered, not knowing what to say. She looked out the window and thought about Robbie, who was a great lover. Flabbergasted, she remained silent.

"Miss Ana Bell, do you want to report any abuse?" the doctor repeated.

"No!" she exclaimed indignantly. "No! I've never been abused, or raped, or cut, or whatever you are assuming here, doctor! I just, literally, I cannot believe what you are telling me."

She paused for a second. "How can I have scars if I have never been cut? I'm sure I would remember, wouldn't I?"

"Well Miss, if what you say is true, then there is only one other explanation."

"Yes, tell me, what is it?" she responded impatiently.

"If you are not trying to protect the perpetrator of this act, which I understand happens when a loved one did something like this to you, or threatened you, but again, if you claim that is not what happened, then we must have a case here of dissociative amnesia."

Ana frowned.

"Amnesia can occur after a serious trauma. It's where the brain goes into a freeze and locks these memories away, deep within your subconscious, so you would have no way of recalling this act."

"What? Is this a joke? No, seriously, you must be kidding me! I come to you to see if I have an infection that causes me pain when I have sex and you start talking about abuse, trauma and this — amnesia? Is this a bad prank?" she retorted angrily as she stood up, turning her back towards him and staring out the window in disbelief.

"Miss, please sit down. We need to take this seriously."

"Pfff, seriously," she scoffed.

He took out the X-ray and pointed to the scan of her pelvic area. "Here, you can clearly see the marks of what looks like a cut. It has left these scars and scar tissue is growing here. I'm not here to trick you."

She turned around to take a look.

"And you're sure you are not mistaking me for somebody else? This is a scan of my womb?"

"Yes, certainly," he responded, his voice cold and direct.

"So, now what?"

"Unfortunately, there is nothing we can do about it. A surgery would only cause more harm. I can prescribe you a lidocaine gel that numbs the pain, but that is all. But more importantly, with amnesia, I would like to refer you to our psychologist and find a way to do hypnotherapy."

"OMG, the joke continues! You're telling me you don't have an actual remedy for my problem, *and* you recommend me seeing a shrink to do hypnosis. Just making sure I'm getting this!" Ana said with some irony.

"Exactly, Miss. Given your lack of memory, it is advised to get your memory back and see what happened. Of course, I can't force you, but I sincerely believe …"

"Well, I believe we are done here, aren't we?" she interrupted him as she stood up, grabbed her purse and stormed out of his office.

"Thank you, but NO thank you!"

KEY CODE: HIDDEN SCARS

7. CHICKEN WINGS

Ana leaned back in her chair, unable to keep her eyes open any longer. She had been hit by a tornado of energy that had entered her head through her crown, as if she received a download straight from the heavens. Her body was too busy processing this incoming Light information and the intensity would knock her out physically.

Her quest for meditation and self-discovery had kept her sane these past months. After her medical leave, she had decided not to return to her interior design job and started working part-time as a barista at the local coffee shop. She struggled to make ends meet but wanted time to visit Robbie and have enough quiet time by herself.

For the last few weeks, she had been struck by energy waves. She blamed it on her meditations, but it happened randomly, often when she was simply relaxing. Little by little, she was becoming more sensitive to the more subtle levels of her experience, like her energy body. But this energy wave felt like a ten on the Beaufort wind force scale! Ana slowed down her breathing with some deep exhales, anchoring herself into her body, feeling her feet on the ground and her pelvic bowl on the chair.

"I'm open to receive this information and I'm open for this to be easy and graceful," she uttered with a smirk, remembering how her higher self had not taken that request into account the previous time. But hey, it couldn't hurt to try again.

The energy wave moved down her neck and spine, into her back. That was unusual. The bottom of her shoulder blades started to hurt on both sides, so she unhooked her bra to give herself some comfort, without any relief. The spots started burning more and more intensely so she sighed aloud, letting off some steam.

"My God, it's like my chicken wings are hurting!"

No clue where that came from, but Ana compared this spot at the bottom of her shoulder blades to chicken wings. The 'why' would forever remain an unsolved mystery.

"*My wings. My wings are returning,*" her inner voice whispered.

As if those words set her chicken wings on fire, Ana clung to the rail of her chair for dear life.

"What on Earth?! Holy Mother!"

As the intensity knocked her out, Ana entered a dreamlike state.

I feel this Angelic Presence dawn upon me,
as if it flies down from the heavens and stops behind me.
It feels taller, bigger, wider than me.
Nothing but a Presence.
A shape of Light, with huge, wide wings,
softly glistening and twinkling in golden white Light.
An Angel indeed.

It feels so familiar,
a sweet sense of recognition.
I feel this Presence envelop me in Light
and bathe me in what I think is Unconditional Love.
It's Here, Now. I can feel it. Right behind me.
And yet, I wouldn't be able to see it with my eyes.

I can rest Here for eternity,
as all thoughts fade away and there is nothing but Love.
I hear a soft voice reverberating in my ears.
Without a doubt, I know:
it's the Angel.

"Beloved, I Am Here with you Now. You have called upon me to resurrect your inner Knowing. Your desire to restore your Remembrance has been felt across time and space."

"The time has come for you to accept your own divine nature, to know yourself beyond being a human, or even a soul, and accept all aspects of yourself."

"I Am Here to reignite your memory through the Remembrance of your own angel wings, for you too are an Angel."

"You have not fallen from the Grace of God. You are the Divine Spark embodied."

"As you invite your own angel wings to come back to your body, you are accepting another aspect of yourself that has long been denied within humanity, and that has caused a split between your God-self and Human-self."

"Your next initiation is to embrace your Angelic Self and evoke the return of your wings."

"Yes, the ache that burns in your physical vessel is the separation ache your body felt when it started Remembering this, even before your mental body picked it up through this message."

"Ultimately, you are invited to see me as you, and you as me. I'm offering myself in this form, as this is where my consciousness resides, in the upper realms of the 11th dimension, yet there's no-thing in between us. So, allow yourself to see us as One."

Ana's willingness to see immediately resulted in the merging of the Angelic Presence with herself. To the physical eye, Ana was just sitting on a chair. But energetically, the Angelic Presence enveloped her completely and no separation, distance or difference could be seen on an ethereal level. One field of Love.

Ana imagined her wings returning and restoring, attaching to the spots she called the chicken wings, a name never to be used again, as it didn't do justice to the majesty of her actual wings.

Wide, white wings
at least 7 feet high and 4 feet wide,
gently moving,
as if a soft breeze was keeping them alive,
always ready to fly.
She had never felt so much support in her back,
as if she literally was being held,
able to move through the world fearlessly.
Remembering the Power of Love,
Her Love.

A big sigh brought her back into her body as she woke from her dream state. With her eyes still closed, she whispered, "I accept my angel wings."

KEY CODE: ANGEL WINGS

8. SCARS FROM A PAST LIFE

Ana recalled her last visit to her previous gynaecologist. She laughed at the memory as she said to herself, "I was such a bitch!" Now, five years later, she sat in front of a spiritual hypnotherapist, finally willing to face all her trauma. The accident had undeniably changed her.

"I don't understand why they have to look like hippies," she thought, "or like a fortune teller coming straight out of a movie." Ana knew it was just her mind being judgmental, as her heart had guided her there to do a past life regression.

But one couldn't deny that MariAh, the hypnotherapist, did look like a gypsy with her dark, curly black hair and olive skin. She wore lots of rings, with ringing bracelets, a long colourful skirt, and even a wine-red headscarf. Only a crystal ball was missing.

Ten minutes later, Ana was lying on the floor, a blanket covering her body, while crystal bowl music played in the background and the room filled with patchouli incense as MariAh's voice guided her to relax.

"Close your eyes and take a deep breath in and out." She assisted Ana into a breathing technique, called the 4-7-8 method, where she needed to breathe in through the nose for 4 seconds, hold her breath for 7 seconds, then breathe out for 8 seconds. The cadence of the breathing pattern took her into a deep relaxation. She was still alert and awake, but simply became an observer.

As MariAh opened the Akashic Records — the astral library of all universal events that have ever happened and will ever happen — and summoned all timelines that needed healing to reveal themselves, the energy started to spin clockwise around Ana. She became formless, as if she was in black space, spiralling down a tunnel of energy waves, falling deeper and deeper into nothingness, until out of nowhere, a scene began to appear, vaguely at first.

Ana heard her own cry as the scene came closer.

A black-haired woman in rags, covered in blood, was surrounded by women who were trying to help her, yet were in a panic as they didn't know what to do. As Ana watched the bloodied woman, who was at least twenty years older than her, she somehow knew "This is me." Then, time moved backwards.

> *It's dark; the middle of the night. The dark-haired woman is asleep.*
>
> *Trotting horses approach and the lights of torches come closer.*
>
> *Men in black storm into the house and pull her from the hay-stuffed bag she was sleeping on, onto the cold floor.*
>
> *"For you have sinned!" one screams.*
>
> *"You filthy whore!" exclaims another man.*
>
> *"You are the devil!"*
>
> *"You slimy seductress."*
>
> *The beasts rip off her clothes and scold her endlessly.*
>
> *"You don't deserve to live."*
>
> *"You witch!"*
>
> *"You sinner!"*
>
> *The smell of brandy surrounds them.*
>
> *Out of the blue, one of the men pulls a knife out of his*

cape and comes closer. Three other men hold her arms and legs wide open. She struggles, but it all happens so fast. Terror paralyses her. It's as though she detaches from her body and becomes like a ghost.
The man with the knife moves slowly yet with precision as he kneels down. With a deep voice filled with utmost disgust, he whispers to her, "This is what we do to creatures who abandon God. You are not worthy to ever bear his child and procreate yourself. You are a sinner, and we aim for you to already live in hell."
"That no man shall EVER AGAIN enter this filthy creature!" he exclaims as he cuts her vagina open.

The pain catapulted Ana all the way back into her body, where she lay on the ground and snapped out of the memory. A deep womb wail left her mouth.

MariAh urged her to lay back down. "It's ok. You are safe. You are here. You can close your eyes again. Keep breathing, Ana." MariAh tried to reassure her as she guided her back into the breathing pattern.

Ana lay back down and cried. Even though she was not the one in pain, it was as if she could feel all of it.

MariAh gently put her hands on Ana's body. "You are back. You are here, in your own body. You are not that memory or trauma. All that is wanted is for you to see this past life memory and feel it in this moment."

Ana had spoken out loud the memory flashes as she received them, as if she was narrating a movie, so MariAh could be the witness.

"As you mentioned," MariAh continued, "you felt like a ghost, and probably energetically left your body as this happened so suddenly. This is a common thing with trauma, and exactly why these past life traumas can manifest physically in this life, as they want to be felt and ultimately, alchemized back into love."

"So, I am going to ask you to dive in with me one more time," MariAh instructed. "The good news is you only have to do it once. Feel it fully and the memory will dissolve. You're a courageous one, Ana. You're almost there. You made it this far. It may hurt. It may feel like you're about to die. But I want you to know that you are here with me, you are safe, and nothing is going to happen. We are just freeing up this trapped trauma by feeling what you couldn't feel back then. Okay? Are you ready?"

Ana nodded, her face showing her suffering, yet her spirit was strong and her determination even stronger than her fear. She wanted to get this over with once and for all. *#clearthatkarma*

The breathing pattern took her back into deep relaxation, and in the blink of an eye she was back at the scene.

> *The man whispers, "... that no man shall EVER AGAIN enter this filthy creature."*

As Ana entered the memory even deeper, her awareness merged with the dark-haired woman.

> *She now sees the man on top of her. She is being pinned to the ground, completely startled and shocked by what is happening.*
> *He pulls his knife and cuts her open.*

Ana cried out loud, as if she was feeling *all* of it. She screamed, and MariAh too had to hold her body down.

The pain in her vagina is excruciating. Yes, she finds herself in hell. Blood streams out and down her thighs.
The pain is so all-consuming she doesn't notice the men leaving. She just screams and cries it out.
They had not only cut into her body, but also into her mind and her soul.
Her sin was simply being a woman. Her punishment was like a penance for crimes she hadn't even committed. The rest of her life would be hell, but she couldn't know how long these scars would last.

Ana screamed her lungs out.

MariAh encouraged her, "Just one more release."

Ana made another wail and gave it her all, and just like that, *#justlikemagic*, the pain left her body. As if the storm had passed, the suffering came to an end.

Ana gently came back into her own body, feeling the after waves of that shocking experience. She had just set in motion the healing process for those wounds and scars — and their impact — to be healed across all lifetimes.

KEY CODE: HEALING PAST LIFETIMES

9. RECLAMATION

Ana woke up on MariAh's floor, ninety minutes later.

"Welcome back, darling. You are here again," MariAh smiled gently.

Ana was not aware of the time. *"Did she watch me like a freak the whole time?"* she wondered, a bit self-consciously.

MariAh poured her a cup of lavender tea, and asked, "So what is it you are here to See?"

Out of nowhere, the answer immediately rolled out of Ana's mouth, even though her mind was still drowsy.

"I am here to reclaim my sexual power. I am a priestess, a witch and a saint. I have served in many temples, and my body has been an offering to God. I am here to Remember my temple lineage throughout history. I have received the codes of the Divine Feminine again. I see how mankind has haunted us and misunderstood the sacredness we hold, because we carry the power of the Ancients, the power of the Gods within our wombs through the ability to birth life — the ultimate human act of creation."

Ana breathed in deeply and continued, "I reclaim my sexual power." Tears streamed down her face, "I reclaim my sexual sovereignty, my sexual wisdom and I reclaim my body."

She declared in crescendo:

I reclaim my body as mine.
I offer it to no man or to no God.
My body is mine Now.
My pleasure is mine Now.
My sexuality is mine Now.
I choose who I want to let inside of me.
It is my birthright. I Remember my free will.
I reclaim my sexual power Now.
In the name of Qadesh and Aphrodite and all Goddesses who offered themselves to God, I set you all Free.
I set All of us free.

MariAh applauded. Ana felt rushes of life force — yeah, that juicy sexual energy — running up her spine. She was sweating, her feet were firmly planted on the floor, and she felt so much determination. She had no clue where all of that just came from, but oh boy, did it feel powerful!

A light sparked in her yoni. The healing had begun, and thus already ended. The scars of her past life would soon begin to fade away and the pain during lovemaking would turn into pure bliss.

Little did she know, she had just wreaked havoc in the upper realms of goddesses and deities, as through the power of her words she had given them the opportunity to free themselves from all previous contracts they had made in the name of love for God.

KEY CODE: RECLAIM OUR SEXUAL POWER

10. ANGELIC PRESENCE

Ana was writing five things she was grateful for in her journal — a short daily practice she did every night before going to bed— when suddenly, she was enveloped by a coolness, even though the windows were closed and the heating was on. *"Strange,"* she thought, as she closed her eyes. Goosebumps ran all the way down her legs.

She once more felt the Angelic Presence, its energy field fully wrapping around hers as a soft caressing. The coolness reminded her of the air in a temple or cathedral. There truly was a mystical flavour to this experience.

Her body started feeling lighter as gentle energy waves moved up and down her arms and legs, tingling her skin and making the little hairs on her arms rise. Her breath slowed and she naturally relaxed.

Remembering her angel wings, Ana imagined them opening and expanding, extending out seven feet beyond her body, gently moving and opening up her energy field even more. She didn't feel as tight in her body as before. It was as if tension naturally released as she relaxed into her own angelic form.

She had forgotten the sweetness of this feeling. Receiving those angel wings had seemed like a crazy dream, so it had become a memory in the back of her mind. But she couldn't deny the feeling, the experience she was having right here, right now. Feeling expanded. Open. Light. Soft. Peaceful. Graceful. Undisturbed.

"Mmm," she moaned, *"people pay therapists and meditation teachers*

to feel this, and here I am at my desk — feeling like an angel." The thought made her smile.

As she tuned into her heart, she began to understand more deeply that there were multiple layers to who she was. The most prominent one was Ana, the one she woke up as every day, basically the main character in the story of her own life. But she truly believed now that she was a soul on a journey, something that would live on even when Ana died. And then there was her higher self, her own All-Knowing and All-Seeing eye, directly connected to her own path, and therefore the best possible guide.

So, could it be true that she also existed as an angel, or that every Being has an angelic form in a higher realm or dimension?

She paused her thoughts. The truth was she would never know, unless she could suddenly see life through the lens of her higher self.

"That would be cool," she thought, as she winked up to the heavens.

Ana wasn't even sure if it mattered. It was easy to drive yourself nuts by thinking about all the metaphysical and multidimensional things. She waved her thoughts away like clouds and enjoyed the serenity and peace she felt as she connected to her wings.

"Real or surreal, this makes me fly high."

KEY CODE: ANGELIC PRESENCE

II. INSIDE THE KING'S CHAMBER

When Tiny saw the invitation of the mystery school, she immediately knew this was her ticket to freedom. Tiny had been following @Ayana on Instagram for a few months now, intrigued by the sense of mystery and magic this woman exuded. Ayana openly talked about her past life memories of living in Egypt and her connection to the temples. She called herself a Mystery Keeper, connected to the lineage of Isis, and also talked a lot about Mary Magdalene and the Sisters of the Rose. It all sounded a bit surreal, so she was excited to meet Ayana in the flesh and find out if she was sincere or just a really good actress.

Ayana had sparked Tiny's interest to visit Egypt. She wanted to see and experience the land of pharaohs for herself. She had been dreaming of riding a camel next to the pyramids and sailing on the Nile, so when Ayana invited her fellow mystery seekers for a ten-day journey 'Unveiling the Secrets of Ancient Egypt,' Tiny didn't hesitate at all.

Tiny had wanted to leave Taiwan for about a year, but had been waiting for the right opportunity. Although she was afraid her family would be devastated and not support her decision to leave the family home, there was no way she would be living there for eternity. She had already disappointed them by not going to university. Instead, she had finished junior college, gained her undergraduate degree in tourism and hospitality, then said goodbye to the classroom once and for all. She had always been a good student who strived to get top grades, but now Tiny was ready to explore life, travel the globe to new places and meet new people. With her undergraduate degree, she could work in hotels all around the world. She didn't have it in her to add another five years at university, but that's not how her father thought about it.

For years, Tiny's family had been saving up every extra Taiwan dollar they had to support their children to go to university. She was the youngest and sometimes felt like she was the 'one too many' that added an extra burden. Her family had sacrificed everything for her. Her parents wouldn't say it out loud, but she could see their hard work and persistence turn into a silent bitterness and depletion that made them grow old faster than nature intended. That Tiny wanted to go her own way was seen as a sign of ungratefulness.

You see, family and tradition are everything in Taiwan. Tiny absolutely loved that her grandmother lived with them, but life there also felt like living in a cage, not to mention she feared her father secretly wanted to force an arranged marriage and soon would start looking for a matchmaker — another outdated tradition that he still held on to.

But how do you escape from a cage that also feels like a comfortable and safe haven? She had felt torn between the expectations of her family and her own longings and lacked the confidence to take the leap. Procrastination, doubt, fears and insecurity all played a part, but this time, the mystery school invitation made her heart skip a beat and she knew she was ready to look those damn fears in the eye and leave them behind in Taiwan.

With a one-way ticket and a large suitcase, Tiny embarked on the adventure of a lifetime, leaving her family behind, with a tinge of remorse and guilt. It was as if another reality full of possibility opened up for Tiny. Life had been small compared to what she now saw unfolding in front of her eyes.

*

The mystery school initiated her into the great mysteries of Ancient Egypt. Walking around in the temples was beyond magic. It was as if she was walking in a movie set, and yet it was here that the great pharaohs and high priests had walked around. How miraculous that thousands of years later she could still walk in the same buildings, their walls filled with the memory of every person that had been there before and touched the same stones.

The turning point for Tiny was a visit into the Great Pyramid. You couldn't simply walk into this giant structure, and tourism was blooming again in the area of Giza. The mystery school had hired a pair of local guides who knew the ins and outs of how to get a private tour inside all the sacred sites. It was no different with their visit to the Great Pyramid — instead of a tour jam-packed with tourists, they got to spend one hour inside the pyramid with only the twelve of them.

Entering the pyramid, they made their way up the Grand Gallery towards the King's Chamber. A guard welcomed them, holding up a big flashlight that spread a dim light across the majestic room. As soon as she entered the chamber, Tiny was impressed by the intensity of the reverberation and resonance within the room made of pure granite.

The guard asked everyone to sit down and turned off his flashlight. All naturally became as quiet as a mouse in the pitch-black dark, no sounds, other than a moving foot here and there. And yet, Tiny felt as if the space was vibrating all around her. The chamber felt alive. She placed one hand on the wall and the tingling in her hand made her think the stone and her hand were communicating through energy.

Tiny had lost all sense of time when the guard gently nudged her and guided her through the dark towards what she soon would call the Time Travel Box. It was a giant black box, made out of more than 3.5 tonnes of red granite, known as the sarcophagus, at the back of the King's Chamber. The guard silently invited Tiny to lay down inside the stone coffer. The granite stone was hard and cold against the back of her body. Solid and grounding.

The sarcophagus was surrounded by at least four other mystery school initiates, who simultaneously started sounding and OHM-ing, as if they knew exactly when to start their harmony. Their sounds penetrated the stone, creating multiple ripples and reverberations within the sarcophagus. Tiny not only heard the sounds, but also felt them as pure vibration. The sound bath dissolved her awareness of her body, of time and space, until all that was left was a delicious symphony of frequencies.

The initiates started repeating a sequence of tones, as if they had been doing this for lifetimes, and very soon, it was as if they had flipped a switch that prepared the Time Travel Box for launching.

KEY CODE: RESONANCE CHAMBER

12. TIME TRAVEL BOX

*My head starts spinning and spinning,
my crown opens up
and my Light Body expands.*

*It's like I'm multiplying in all directions,
ready to be launched into …
I don't know where.*

*I take a deep breath,
as I continue to feel the sounds penetrate my whole being.
As I breathe out,
in a flash,
I am no longer laying in the black box,
but I find myself back in time …*

Midday, Egypt. The temple complex at Dendera is in full construction. I look around and see life play out in a strange combination of slow motion and fast forward. It's as if I can read the energy patterns and dynamics playing out here simply by witnessing this scene. I understand how life works. I understand what is going on.

I know the Dendera Zodiac is meticulously being sculpted in the ceiling of the temple of Hathor. I know who has taken over the throne and the secrets that are kept hidden within the temples. I know the poverty and injustice the slaves endure, and simultaneously can sense the joy in the children's hearts, for as long as they can retain their innocence. It's like I have become clairvoyant and each scene reveals its secrets to me.

"*Why am I here?*" I wonder. "*Why am I seeing this?*"

My questions instantaneously change the scene, and in the blink of an eye, I find myself in the corner of a kitchen where an Egyptian woman is preparing a meal.

I pick up that she has 'lost her power,' yet I am not sure what that means. It feels as if she has been kicked off the throne. The woman is trying to hide here as a maid in the house, yet she knows she can't stay here too long.

Oh, my — this is Cleopatra! The forgotten story of Cleopatra!

She went into the history books as the lover of Julius Caesar and the last pharaoh in Egypt, yet few know what really happened to her when Octavian took over the throne. For centuries, myths have spread the story that she poisoned herself.

Cleopatra had always been in touch with her psychic abilities, so she sensed a presence in the room. She looked up in my direction and I knew I couldn't hide, even though I was invisible and only my awareness appeared.

"I can *feel* you," she said with suspicion. "Make yourself known. Speak your intent." She spoke Aramaic, yet I understood as if it were English.

"*I am simply here to See.*" The thought travelled from my awareness into hers. Her stare became even stronger, as if she could actually see someone stand in front of her.

"Reveal yourself!" Cleopatra commanded.

"*I am You. You are Me,*" I paused, "*I am a future aspect of your-self, here to witness and Remember who I Am. I came to see when and where*

I first gave away my power, so I may gain greater understanding of my own journey."

I had no control over what was being exchanged and learned about the details as the story played out in my inner eye.

"My future self, ha — what better time to come find me than when I am down on my knees and defeated by fate! How I would have loved to show you the majesty and abundance I created, the nightly feasts I was known for, the beauty that once surrounded me. Yet you choose to see me in my own inglorious demise. Your own demise," she sneered bitterly, "yet that is how we shall learn. See what you need to See and then take off! This memory will last for eternity, and I don't want to extend it any longer."

Her comment doesn't make me flinch, and I do See all I need to See. I don't really understand what's going on, but somehow, I needed to see this to understand something about Cleopatra, and thus myself.

"I still don't get how I gave away my power, or how she was kicked off the throne." My thoughts shift from the scene and take me a few months back in time.

✱

Cleopatra is still on the throne, lavishing in her beauty, revelling in her power, and enjoying all who literally lay at her feet and dance to whatever tune she sings. She knows how to play the chords of each instrument she possesses, and her instruments are the humans around her. She is blinded by her own greed for this lustrous life and the power that comes with it. Since Julius Caesar's assassination, she has stopped caring about what happens outside the walls of her queendom and is just living out her fantasies.

But greed is blinded by power, and so it happened that an insidious Stranger was tired of standing by and watching Cleopatra being caught up in her fantasy world instead of extending their world dominion. He craved to be in power and fantasised about Egypt once again becoming the mighty empire it once was. Instead of letting the Romans chip away at their land, he was determined to return Egypt to its full glory and make his ancestors proud.

He knew the only way in was through Cleopatra's heart and her sexual fantasies. A man who is shooting directly for his aim will not miss an arrow, so soon he was the one lying at her feet, experiencing a whole new world of pleasure he had never been part of before. However, his secret mission was more sacred to him, so even though his own sexual cravings were more than met at her feasts, he stayed on top of his game.

Soon, he began to sow jealousy, greed and mistrust among her servants. The tension grew, yet Cleopatra had no idea of the insidious snake venom that had entered her fantasy world. Blinded by his charm, she trusted the Stranger to make amends as she continued to drink her golden elixir. She wasn't clear-headed and continued her never-ending party, rather than taking charge of what mattered.

When the insidious Stranger went to talk to the head council of Egypt, they all agreed the time had come for their queen to step away from the throne. They all knew her fury too well, so their only strategy was to plan a coup. Everyone was aware of it but Cleopatra herself, oh, and some of her lustful boys.

One man was charged with the duty of killing Cleopatra in her sleep, but as the assassin snuck up on her in the early morning — the only time she would sleep — he hesitated for a moment too long, enthralled by her beauty, and as she opened her eyes and gasped for air, facing the knife he held, he fell on his knees and begged for mercy.

As he confessed to her about the coup, she knew they wouldn't stop coming after her, and Julius was no longer around to come and save the day. She had only two options: to be found dead on her bed or to flee and escape this destined demise. Her choiceless choice was to leave everything behind. And so, she ran away in the early morning.

*

In an instant, Tiny flashed back into the Time Travel Box. At superfast speed, she recalled her journey into Ancient Egypt and meeting Cleopatra. She couldn't wipe away the feeling of it all being real. Mind-blowing, yet so real. How could it be that she was Cleopatra? And what would people think if she even dared to share this out loud?

The tones started to fade and the silence penetrated her ears, maybe even louder than the toning. Just the pure sound of silence. Her body was lit up from her travel journey into the past, yet chilly from laying in the cold granite box.

Soon, she would find out she wasn't the only one who had travelled inside the box. She would discover this was indeed a Time Travel Box, a secret known by the ancient mystery schools and consciously used to see throughout space and time. The pharaohs who used it knew how to operate it and were even able to peek into their future to adjust their decisions — not that fate could be turned around, yet they could prepare for what was to come and allow their destiny to play out accordingly.

There was something mind-boggling about the experience. Tiny couldn't be more opposite to Cleopatra. From the most introverted to the most extroverted. From the most altruistic to the most self-indulgent.

Power was a foreign word to Tiny. She had been taught that was something of men and of the elders. A young woman in power — it seemed unimaginable and had never even crossed her mind.

Tiny realised Cleopatra didn't really give her power away. It was as if she had no other choice but to flee. And yet, she did end up in a completely powerless position. The shame and the loss of everything she had built left a deep wound in Cleopatra and a deep-rooted belief to not ever again seek power, as it will only be taken away. She made an oath with her soul to never, ever experience that amount of shame again. She hoped people would remember her as the great Cleopatra and prayed people would never find out the truth of her story and demise. Her will was strong, and her secret remained.

At night, Tiny shared her experience with Ayana. She didn't feel comfortable enough to share it with all the other initiates. Ayana, with her wide and bright green eyes, listened carefully. She didn't blink an eye, nor did she appear to question Tiny for one moment.

"I am recognising myself in Cleopatra. I can see myself in her, even though we couldn't be more opposite. Yet, I *Know* her. I *Feel* her — how she lost everything she had built. I can feel the shame she went through, but also her greatness. I can feel how her despair created a disgust towards power. She never wanted to go through that again."

"Are you willing to clear these past karmic bonds and oaths, my dear?"

"How so?" Tiny asked timidly.

"Well," Ayana said, "you told me Cleopatra made an oath to never ever be in a position of power again. She wasn't just speaking about her own life. She created an oath that rippled out throughout her whole soul's journey. She made an oath to never ever, meaning in no other lifetime, be in power again."

"Now this has been revealed to you, you have the opportunity to clear this, to make it undone and to free yourself, to free up your energy and to reclaim your own power."

Ayana chuckled, "I can see what you think, my dear, no worries. It's not that you have to become the next Cleopatra. You have already lived that life. But right now, your power, your life force energy, is bound by this oath. It's as if you have not been fully free to live the life you desire due to this past oath. What power means today is very different from what it meant thousands of years ago. And most importantly, it will be up to you to find out and discover what being in your power means to you, Tiny."

One couldn't have come up with a more heroic journey than to ask Tiny, a most introverted creature, to step back into her power. And yet, there was something inside of her that was curious to know what power really meant. She had come to have a deep trust in Ayana, even though they had only been together for about a week, so she agreed to clear the past oath.

Ayana cast out several powerful invocations, while Tiny just sat in front of her with closed eyes as she imagined a stream of energy, her life force and her power, coming back into her body and settling into the base of her pelvic bowl. The oath had been broken, and even Cleopatra's spirit smiled as Tiny opened up a new timeline for power to be experienced in a different way.

KEY CODE: TIME TRAVEL

13. Meeting Beyond the Veil

It happened more and more often that when Ana dozed off, whether in the early morning, late afternoon or evening, she would travel in dream state and receive another mysterious message. While her body was in deep relaxation and her mind became more like an observer, she was open to receiving the messages without much resistance.

> *I find myself in the middle of a forest*
> *with large, dark green pine trees all around me.*
>
> *I walk into an open spot with no trees,*
> *where the sun kisses my skin*
> *as I gaze up and see the bright sky.*
>
> *Out of nowhere,*
> *a giant silver-framed mirror appears*
> *in front of me as I look back down.*
>
> *I am drawn towards the mirror.*
> *Gently, I place one foot in front of the other.*
> *My bare feet touch the earth,*
> *feeling the fresh dew on the moss.*

I feel peaceful,
a thought-free stillness,
while my body moves forward
until I stand right in front of the mirror.

As I gaze into the mirror
and into my own eyes,
the contours of my body become sharper,
the background fades away
and I see my-self.

The eyes I am looking into
are radiant,
filled with curiosity
and inviting me.

A soft smile emerges on my face.
I see her beauty,
my own beauty.

I lift my hand to touch the mirror
and as my fingertips touch the glass,
the mirror shatters
into a thousand pieces.

Crystal clear
pieces of glass
turning into dust.

The mirror disappears.
She is now in front of me.

I can still see her contours,
yet the only thing left of her
is a mist of soft blue light
in a humanoid form.

As my hand reaches out,
my fingertips touch hers.

A gentle touch,
like a subtle energy
that softly tickles my fingertips.

She doesn't speak,
yet I hear her voice.

"Here we meet."

"I want you to know that
this is real.
This is not just a dream."

"We encounter
in the astral realms,
where you can meet
more of yourself."

"I carry a Peace and Stillness
that is like water to your fire.
It creates more balance
and restores your body's well-being."

"I am Here
to help you Remember
who you are,
who we are."

"I come from the angelic realms.
I appear in this form to you,
as I hold less density
and I have no physical form."

"We are a part
of the same."

"We are a part
of the same."

"We are a part
of the same."

The words still echoed in Ana's head as she woke from yet another dream.

"*We are a part of the same.*"

It felt like a riddle that wanted to be solved, but she didn't see the punch line yet.

KEY CODE: MEETING BEYOND THE VEIL

14. DOCTOR! DOCTOR!

It was a Friday night, not in the park, but another evening at the hospital. Ana had just finished reading another poem out of Rumi's *Little Book of Life* and stood up to reach across the bed to kiss Robbie's forehead.

"Oh, Robbie, how handsome you are with your black hair. Oh ... wait ... I see you're getting a few grey ones. How is it you're still getting older without getting to live more life? You are like a sleeping prince, and every day I hope I am the one who can kiss you awake, but I'm not gonna bring a frog in here, you know." Ana was used to talking out loud to herself, so she spoke to Robbie as if he could hear her and didn't mind if anyone saw her babble as she enjoyed her own spontaneous nature.

She held his hand and closed her eyes. For a minute, she sat in silence with him and connected to his soul.

"Robbie, I know you can hear me. I know you can feel me. When are you coming back, my Love?" she asked, without awaiting his response, "I want to start a whole new life with you. I want a second chance with you. I still believe we are meant to ..."

She felt something!

She felt it move! It may have been just one phalanx of his finger, but she was sure she felt it move in her hand. She ran out of his hospital bedroom and the whole patient hallway could hear her calling out hysterically, "Doctor! Doctor! He is moving!"

✯

It took another few weeks for Robbie to wake up fully, but he did, surely and steadily. For the first few weeks, he would just sit up and stare at Ana with his blue eyes, as she continued to read his favourite poems. Even though he wasn't speaking yet, she could stare back at him for hours, at least, metaphorically speaking.

She could get lost in his eyes, his deep blue ocean eyes. They invited her into a state of stillness. She wondered if they had ever stared into each other's eyes that long before? Maybe early on, when they first fell in love, but then she would often turn her gaze away when she felt her cheeks begin to blush.

This eye gazing was taking their connection to a whole other level, even without words, and her love for Robbie was growing day by day. Somehow, she felt fully seen. She could not confirm what Robbie was seeing, thinking or feeling, or if he could still do any of those things, but again, it felt as if he could see right through her and knew the woman she was becoming.

KEY CODE: EYE TO EYE

15. TIME TO MOVE ON

The big day had come. Ana hadn't felt this amount of stress in a long time. Robbie was coming home today, to live with her in the tiny house she was renting just outside of Mount Shasta.

Ana had no idea how it would be to live together. Even though she had known Robbie for years, it felt as if she would be living with a stranger. Just like her, Robbie too had changed.

To Ana, it seemed as if the dust had fallen away and a clear spark had returned. She had already witnessed this in Robbie's eyes, but it also came through in his movements and words. He was fully present in each moment and spoke so clearly, directly and truthfully, without beating around the bush. Perhaps Robbie didn't want to waste any more time in his life either. For sure, 'Friday nights at the park' was a thing of the past for them both. Ana felt they were finally getting into a real-ationship, instead of just having fun, hanging out together and having sex.

"It's time to go, my Love," Robbie said with a gentle smile. His blue eyes made her heart pound again and she giggled with delight for him to come home. "Let's go, babe," she replied happily and off they went.

As they left the hospital and walked to her car, a white butterfly passed by, seemingly unnoticed, yet definitely registered by their subconscious brains.

KEY CODE: REAL-ATIONSHIP

16. THE WITCH HUNT

Tiny woke up from a nightmare, her head at the foot end of the bed and her body drenched in sweat. She didn't quite remember what had just happened, but she did know she feared for her life.

Tiny was longing to share her art with the world. Since her travels to Egypt, she had been writing about her adventures in the form of story and poetry, art forms that didn't seem so popular anymore, but she loved to weave words together in a miraculous flow that astounded the readers and moved something within them. Whether surprise or emotion, just the idea of evoking something in the reader lit Tiny up.

But her insecurity had kicked in again. Her longing to share her art and be seen was overshadowed by a much bigger fear that kept her in hiding. Every time she thought of sharing it with someone, her throat felt blocked, as if she was about to be strangled.

She carried with her multiple notebooks full of poems and unfinished stories, but all of it was kept hidden, for her eyes only. And yet, the desire encoded within her art to be of service to the heart of her readers wouldn't stop nudging her to do something with it.

She called Ayana, who was not only a Mystery Keeper, but who also offered past lifetime regressions.

Tiny shared about her challenge, and before she realised what was happening, she had her eyes closed and Ayana was guiding her to look into the origin of the fear and guiding her way back in time.

It was just like when she was lying in the Time Travel Box. In a flash, she was catapulted back in time, this time deep into the Middle

Ages, the era of kings and castles in Europe.

> *She saw herself standing at the beam, the strop around her neck, about to be hung up, along with two other women.*
> *No mercy was granted. She would die a painful death.*
> *The sin: witchery.*
> *An unforgivable sin at that time.*

Multiple flashes popped up, one after the other. Short bursts of memory passed by, fleeting, yet just enough to get the gist of it.

> *Women being burned at the stake.*
> *Hidden meetings with other women in a cave in the forest.*
> *Dancing under the moonlight around a fire.*
> *Sexual initiations in the temples with men from all walks of life coming to quench their sexual thirst.*

> *She was hunted.*
> *She was prosecuted.*
> *She was hung.*
> *She was killed.*
> *She was banned.*
> *She was hunted down.*
> *She was drowned.*
> *She was repelled.*
> *She was crushed with stones.*
> *She was abandoned.*

It seemed like an endless story that repeated itself over and over again, and then the most dreadful memory came into sight again.

A lifetime as a medicine woman, in tune with the alchemy of nature and in touch with the cycles of the moon and the sun. Initiating the young women of the village into the mysteries of the womb. Hunted down by a huntsman who slit her throat for speaking her truth.

The repeated traumas were still imprinted in her cellular memory and had ingrained the belief 'It is not safe to speak my truth. My life is in danger when I speak my truth.'

The revelation of this information made Tiny cough incessantly, as if there was something she needed to spit out from her chest.

"You are releasing, dear, it's okay. Cough as much as you need to. Imagine you are coughing up all the trauma, all the fear that got injected and projected onto you that was not yours. Cough it up and out. Better out than in," Ayana supported her.

The coughing continued for at least ten more minutes before she could breathe freely again.

"Now, let's release the strop that energetically still hangs around your neck."

Tiny touched her neck and couldn't feel anything. She had carried it her whole life, so she couldn't even tell it was there. Ayana evoked some clearing energy and commanded the energetic strop to be released and ejected from Tiny's field. "May all that needs to be seen come to the forefront now, so that this energy can be released and return to its original state."

Tiny started yawning and felt a subtle energy shift around her neck. The strangling feeling had left for sure, but it even felt as if there was more space around her neck. She yawned again and naturally made some moaning sounds.

"Yes, that's it. Claim back that voice, my dear. Now, while you are still in Egypt, I believe it would be wise to reclaim your voice. You are doing it now; you have already done it. But go out into the desert, and surrounded by its vast stillness, start to sing, sound and tone. Make as much sound as you can. And if you will, find your own tone."

"My tone?" Tiny asked.

"Yes, your tone. It's the song of your soul — the sound of your Essence, your unique vibration. When you tone in tune with it, your whole body will light up and feel just like the King's Chamber of the Great Pyramid. You'll feel your whole body vibrate. You are ready now to unlock this key."

"This key?"

"The key to your Sound. Every key holds information, wisdom and frequencies for you to Remember, discover and activate in your Being. You are now opening your throat more, and you'll find your tone will be of great assistance on your path. That's all you need to know for now, my dear. Just go out in the desert and sing your song. The bird doesn't think about what song to sing, it just whistles, so go and do that."

KEY CODE: RECLAIM YOUR VOICE

17. FINDING HER TONE

Later that evening, under the night sky, Tiny tuned into her heart and whispered, "Finding my own song, finding my tone, oooh, let me not think too much about it. I just want to feel it. Let me just sing and tone."

She gathered her confidence and started sounding in the open air of the desert.

♪ *Aaaaaaah*
♪ *Ooooooooh*
♪ *LaLaDiDaDiDaDa*

Playing with her voice, toning up and down, Tiny got so lost in the act of using her voice that she forgot she had the aim to find her own tone. She just sang her heart out. And as she did, she opened her throat even more — energetically — and allowed the energy to flow more easily up and down in her body, connecting it all the way down into her roots and up into her third eye.

The notes were coming out clearer and stronger. As her sound connected to her womb, there was more punch behind it, and she could hold the notes for longer. As she continued, she started producing overtones and sang in ways she had never sung before. It felt so freeing to use her voice like this. It reminded her of *Moana*, the Disney movie that inspired her to roam the world, and now she felt just as free as she had imagined.

She hit a tone she hadn't made before that created shivers up and down her spine. Immediately, she Remembered, "My tone!"

Tiny tried to reproduce it and missed. Trying again, a little higher, she hit it. Another wave of energy surged up her spine. Another try, louder this time. The energy waves continued as she produced the note. It felt like it cleared her whole Being into a crystal clarity she hadn't known before, while fully filling her up with her own energy. Oh, what a yumminess!

She took another big breath before making her tone again:

♪ *Hoooooooooooeeeeeeeeeh*

She could clearly feel the energy, just like ocean waves rising and rolling in and around her. She was bathing in the energy and didn't want to stop singing.

"I believe I have found my tone."

KEY CODE: THE SONG OF YOUR SOUL

18. NEW EYES TO SEE

Robbie slowly opened his eyes from what felt like a lifelong sleep. The first thing he saw were her green eyes, then her long, curly red hair.

"*Ana,*" he thought, yet no sound left his mouth.

Her eyes smiled back at him as she started an ecstatically joyful dance, kissing him all over his face. He heard her words, yet they didn't really compute. He mostly *felt* her. He felt her energy, her joy, her ecstasy, and her love.

He stared into her eyes, almost as if he saw them for the first time, while her irises drew him in and reminded him of how timeless their connection was. It was the first time he could really see Her, *all* of Her. Ana as the woman he had known, Ana as the woman she was now, and who she was before she was born as Ana.

Her eyes revealed the story of her soul, and without seeing the details of the movie playing out, it was as if he could see the whole journey her soul had been on, her past lifetimes, and even glimpses of her future to come. He knew they had been journeying together before, and even though the details remained a mystery, a deep Knowing anchored into his heart. This woman was his life partner, a part of his destiny.

She stared right back into his eyes. Time stopped ticking and the Earth stopped spinning. Every-one and every-thing faded away. There was nothing left but this eternal moment where two souls meet. Their eyes were locked, exchanging a love beyond words, information without sound, and memories of long-forgotten times. They became selflessly engaged with the moment, fully present, drinking in their love.

The thought, *"We are so different, yet I see myself in Her/Him,"* passed through both their minds.

A deep recognition settled into their hearts.

A Remembrance of their connection beyond this lifetime. Silent, yet felt.

Robbie tasted Ana's tears, received her words, loved her kisses and enjoyed the way her energy enveloped him when she came to visit. He especially enjoyed it when she read his favourite lines of a Rumi poem.

> *Beloved, am I the seeker or the sought?*
> *Until I am I, You are another.*
> *There is no place for 'You' and 'I' in unity.*

His communication with the outer world remained limited for a while after being in a coma, yet Robbie was alert, awake and present like never before. He even felt his body in a completely different way, as if he'd always been asleep, numb, and somehow disconnected, especially from the lower half of his body.

The way he engaged with the outer world was more connected, experiencing every particle that has turned into matter, registering all sensations, and feeling them as the energy waves and frequency patterns that they are. He had become more sensitive, and even though it would be overwhelming to some, Robbie felt a deep comfort and stability by feeling so interconnected with All of Life around him. Somehow, he felt more like himself.

Robbie underwent his recovery in utmost peace, with patience and without resistance to what is. His glimpse of life after death had changed his life's perspective for the better.

KEY CODE: TIMELESS CONNECTION

19. A SPARK OF LIGHT

Robbie didn't catch what was happening. He just tried to grab his water bottle, sure he had left it on the floor of the passenger's side. He needed to hydrate, as he felt lightheaded after drinking a few too many beers.

The guardrail showed up too quickly, with no chance to brake. They broke through the barrier and crashed hard into the ditch in just seconds. Robbie blacked out as his head hit the steering wheel.

Nothing.

Nothing happened.
Nothing showed up.

Just eternal blackness.

He was Here.
Aware.

Yet it didn't feel as if he was still in a body.
He had no senses to give him any input.

Even though he was no-body,
it felt as if he started spinning and moving,
spiralling in and out, up and down,

until he lost all sense of direction.

The movement lasted for eternity,
until the blackness faded,
replacing itself with what 'felt like'
Eternal Light,
because he had no eyes to see.

Its brightness
penetrated his whole Being,
or whatever was left of it.

It enveloped him, surrounded him,
washed over him, carried him.
There was no difference
between within or without.

All there was,
was Light.

Maybe He was the Light?

The memory of Robbie
was like a long distant memory
in a faraway time and space.

Here,
He Simply Be
Eternally.

His time as Light, however long or short it may have lasted, washed his body, mind and soul clean. It was as if it had purified his understanding of himself and life, and his earlier priorities as an early twenty-something-year-old man had been replaced by deeper desires that sprang from deep within his Being. What had been important no longer was, and what had seemed futile, now became his life's North Star.

As he returned from the Light into his body, he brought with him an understanding of the preciousness of life. He would no longer take his Earth life for granted, ever, and understood that life as Robbie was only a blip within the vastness of creation.

Yet, he now had the ability to be fully present to it, and through his awareness, he could drink it in fully. Every moment in time — irreplaceable — as every moment is as unique as a snowflake and will never return, but become a memory that can be picked up for a while, only to be lost within a sea of infinite memories.

He was committed, without needing a commitment, to not drink his life away. A deeper devotion had sprouted within him, to live a life with no regrets. That meant to live out his destiny.

Never ever had he pondered what destiny could mean, or if he had one and what it could be. But now, his whole life naturally seemed to be fuelled towards living out his destiny and bringing everything he could to the table to fulfil it. He wasn't here just for earthly pleasures; his life was a part of his soul's journey.

He didn't need words to explain it, or to even understand it. There was a fuel, a spark of light within him that he intuitively knew had the coordinates necessary to live out his destiny. The direction he was headed was already laid out.

Ultimately, he knew he couldn't even screw this up. He tried that once and that led to the crash. Life would course-correct if he went off track. Living his destiny was inevitable. All of Life, the whole Universe, conspired to make that happen. Not just for him, for everyone. It's just that most people didn't answer the phone call of their higher self until they, well, crashed, he guessed.

He sensed that Ana, too, had become a different version of herself. He didn't know if she had spent time within that eternal light, but her eyes had the same spark he recognized within himself. The way she moved, patiently sat beside him and read his favourite poem day after day, just the simple fact that she was sticking around told him she too had become more of Her-Self. And maybe, just maybe, she too Remembered their bond beyond the simple love affair they had shared before.

KEY CODE: DESTINY

20. CALLING OUT

Another night under the stars. Another tear welling up in her eye.

Tiny called upon her higher self. She had never communicated with Her-Self in this way, but her time in the mystery school had introduced her to so many new spiritual practices that made her relate to herself and the world in a more mystical and magical way.

She had set sail from Taiwan to Egypt, but now she felt stranded in the Sinai Desert, wondering what she was actually doing with her life. None of it made sense. Where would she go next? She didn't want to go back home, nor stay in Egypt, but she didn't know much about the world. She felt astray and needed a sign, some answers or some clarity.

She assumed her higher self would have the answer, could see the greater plan of her life and set all of this play in motion, so she was convinced, *"It knows what is best for me and what is not."*

Tiny's understanding of higher self was still limited, and she naively believed it would work just as efficiently as Google, so she was highly disappointed when she realised she couldn't just type in a question and get the answer. She wasn't even sure if her higher self could hear her. She hadn't heard or received any answers yet. When she tried to get clear on her next steps, the only thing that popped up was 'follow your heart,' but that sounded like a fortune cookie message and she brushed it off as just her mind talking.

Another night went by. She started reminiscing about her life in Taiwan. The hot desert made her miss the humidity and warm climate. She missed the sounds of thunderstorms and ocean waves.

She thought back to how she used to join her mother and grandmother at the fish market near the harbour, where she had learned how to cut fish and even make *Tian Bu La*, traditional fish cakes from white fish fillets that were deep-fried until golden brown. Her grandmother would always remind her, "Man man chi," which meant, "Savour your food slowly," in Mandarin.

Tiny grew up in Chenggong, a traditional fisherman's village in East Taiwan. It wasn't without reason her family was known as the Ocean Tribe. The Yang family cared for their boat as if it was their most precious possession. Her father still fished with a harpoon and was against the new fishing technologies that were being imported, using industrial, plastic nets to catch fish.

"Fishing is an honour. To fish with a harpoon requires focus and effort," her father said. One day, he caught a swordfish with his harpoon. It was a symbol of pride, and the day broke out into a feast. She knew this was a precious memory as their fishing lineage was destined to die due to overfishing, which had become a serious problem in the waters around Taiwan.

Just for a moment, Tiny wished to be back at home with her grandmother, who would serve the most delicious snacks until she couldn't eat any more. But going home somehow felt like going back, instead of moving forward on her path. With a touch of nostalgia in her heart, she fell asleep.

The next day, Tiny spent the night under the stars again. She truly was a night owl, wandering and wondering what was next, but the heat had made her feel tired and brought her into a sweet surrender of giving up.

She was lying on the sand in 'savasana,' the yogic dead man pose, with her head towards the sky and eyes wide open. The wind blew softly, wiping her thoughts away as if she gave them one-by-one to the wind and imagined them drifting by like speech bubbles in a comic book. She looked up to the stars and felt her heart connect and reach out to the cosmos. And then, it just happened.

Tiny felt a Presence that felt familiar, yet new. It didn't feel as if someone else was with her, it just felt like there was more of her, all around her, as if this Presence whispered words into her ears.

"I am Here. I always am and always have been."

A gentle breeze passed by.

Tiny felt peaceful, unmoved by the Presence, as she was One with it. Without asking a question, she received the answer to what she had been pondering.

"Go where your heart leads you. Follow that inner pull that has brought you here. It knows its destination."

She closed her eyes and placed her hands on her heart.

"Follow what gives you joy, follow what brings you excitement and follow what opens up your whole Being. Find that subtle voice within that Knows, that is here and that speaks to you now. There is a divine simplicity you can be in if you follow a flow that does not know resistance, because it trusts what appears and shows up in your life. Don't question your desires as they are God-given and allow yourself to be in a flow that carries you as a light feather across the world. You don't want to go home, and it is not time yet to go back. There is a new home waiting for you and more adventure to come. Be open to the mystery and follow your heart, that is all you can do."

With every word, Tiny felt more relaxed.

"Trust your inner gut, that instinctive Knowing that immediately speaks, faster than lightning, without making sense. Stop trying to make sense and be a 'good girl.' Your destiny is outside of the limits of your comfort zone and outside the perimeters of what a good Taiwanese woman is supposed to be like. Continue to step into what is new and *unknown. You have faced this discomfort and fear before as you left your home, and so, you can do it again. The more you do, the easier it becomes and the more fun it becomes, until eventually, you know nothing else."*

Tiny lay on her back and allowed the message to land. Wow. She had never received so much clarity from within herself. It sounded very wise, or at least, exactly what she needed.

It wasn't too hard to remember. *"Just follow your heart. Just follow your heart, Tiny."* It was more than just fortune cookie advice.

With her hand on her heart, she fell asleep, the soothing silence of the desert guiding her into a dream state. It's here she would be anchoring these insights into her Being, and in her dream, she would live out what she had just been told and experience it first hand, as a primer for her external reality. Little did she know, it would be her final night in the desert as the next adventure was about to knock on her door.

KEY CODE: HIGHER SELF

21. Like a House of Cards

Wouldn't life always stay a mystery?
One that we're all trying to figure out and understand?
It seems like everyone is trying to grasp HOW to do life, because if we don't do it well, if we don't win, if we don't succeed and we fail, then …
Then what, actually?!
Then you go to hell?!
Then you fall flat on your face?!
Then you have no clue what to do next?!

Robbie was having a tough day. He was still adjusting to being back in the world. He couldn't stand how people were caught in a web of illusions. He had been no different, but now he was looking at life through a different lens and just needed to get his thoughts out on paper.

We're trying so hard to win at life.
Trying to get it right.
Trying to succeed.
Trying to find success as if it's the pot of gold at the end of the rainbow.
Trying to grasp for control and cling onto safety by getting a job, by buying a house, by getting married or being in a relationship.
And yeah, sure, if you have a job, you know what's going to pay the bills next month. And yeah, if you get married, you know who you are going to wake up with the next day.
But honestly, even that's an illusion. False certainty.
Because there is no way anyone can tell for sure if the sun will come up again tomorrow — we just assume it will.
Or that our heart keeps on beating — we just take it for granted.
Or that our loved ones will be there by our side — we just ignore the fact that their life is as fragile as the petals of a rose.
My glimpse of heaven showed me how little we know.
But I have learned that no-thing outside of me can give me safety.
The only thing I am certain about is the simple fact that … I exist.
That I Am. My breath is the proof of my existence.

I Am Here. And I Know I have my own back.
That no matter what, having a job or no job, having a home or no home, having a relationship or not, I've got myself.
I have survived a lot of suffering and I am still breathing.
I got this.

That's what I can be certain about.
But your life — that's just like a house of cards.
With one blow, your certainty can be taken away and all safety is lost.
How did we become so blind and forget that no safety can be found in a contract, in a brick wall or in a golden ring?
All of these are temporary anyway.

Everybody tries to hold their house of cards together, and meanwhile, forgets to look up to the sky and enjoy the sunlight, forgets how giant this universe is and how tiny we are.
Just bringing some relativity to our daily drama.

People get faced with this in their life when they hit a brick wall.
When someone dies. When someone gets a burn-out, depression, a disease or midlife crisis.
But otherwise, most people just live in pure denial.
In pure denial of not knowing what the fuck they are doing with their life.
In pure denial that they have no clue what is next.
That life is an absolute mystery.
That the future is always unknown.

Trying to keep it together by making plans, setting goals, having a vision of what the future needs to be like.
But humans can't predict when destiny will knock on the door.
When that catalyst shows up.
When you're about to lose someone you love.
When it's time for your next soul lesson.

Life is full of surprises. And that ain't always pleasant.
It is a full-on mystery.

Be honest with yourself and face it ...
You are afraid of the dark.
You are afraid of the unknown.
You fear the void.
You fear not knowing what is next.
You fear facing the truth.
And to not feel those fears, you live in your own house of cards built with bricks of illusions.

What will it take for people to see how stuck they really are in their life?!

Robbie threw his pen down, held his head in his hands and let out a heavy sigh. He was in a judgmental mood and tried to tame his frustration, but however far he looked back in history, he couldn't find a time — at least according to the history books — where fear and lack, greed and competition, injustice and power games had not been part of daily life. Humanity had been lost for centuries. He didn't know what this human experiment was set up for, but he doubted if it was actually working. Robbie longed for a different world. He believed that Earth could be a place where all living Beings could thrive. He knew it was possible. It even seemed simple.

And yet, today, he wasn't feeling very hopeful. The age of independence had created a selfish race. If you were to hand people an alternative on a golden platter, most would resist giving up their phones, giving up their fake social lives or giving up their houses full of stuff they didn't need. Most people just seemed to care about themselves instead of the human family, let alone the planet as our home.

Robbie hoped he was wrong. He just needed to allow these thoughts to come up, to see through his own judgments, and ultimately, allow his deeper truth to pierce through his own beliefs. That would reveal what he was invited into next.

KEY CODE: BUSTING THROUGH ILLUSIONS

22. THE DESIGN

Topic: Imprinting the Six-Crystal

It was in the year 1988 that the design was imprinted into six different astrological constellations. The original Six-Crystal, resting in the higher realms, was set to explore its next iteration through a 3D experience on Earth — entering a world of duality where it would separate, only to Remember its wholeness and Oneness.

The template would split into six Beings. Each would embody an aspect of the whole while, just like a fractal, carrying the Six-Crystal deep within their core.

Each would have a specific blueprint and a unique activation sequence that would unlock in their DNA, while all would share the same highest intention to embody their Oneness as a collective on Earth, to move as One, be as One and live as One while incarnated in their human forms.

It was an endeavour that had not happened on Earth since time immemorial.

Collectives had formed and there had been many trials to form resonant groups of twelve, yet they had always centred around a 13th Head. That was a different design and constellation, mostly remembered through Jesus and his twelve apostles.

This new iteration was one where all were equal aspects, carrying 60° of the whole, together closing the circle of 360°.

They were meant to go beyond any dynamics of separation,

hierarchy or comparison, and to bring their own unique gifts and abilities forward, aka activate 60°, in order to make the whole thrive and operate at its highest potential. Given they each carried different aspects, they were naturally complementary and would benefit from co-creating and exchanging.

As the Six-Crystal split into six aspects, first on an ethereal level, each held a unique Essence that would be reflected in their personality traits and could be interpreted through their astrological constellation of their birth time.

Each would drop in at a different point in time, with just a few Earth years difference, at different spots on Earth. Based on their design, the details like birth location, birth vessels (aka parents) and environments became clear.

Multiple markers were placed on the timelines of their lives. Just like the notes on a music sheet represent the exact frequency and exact timing, so too were both their individual and collective timelines orchestrated. This is how divine orchestration was set in motion.

Due to the gap between the higher realms and the actualisation of it in 3D, no one could foresee how the human aspects would relate to the Veil of Forgetfulness, nor what they would do with their free will.

To keep the highest intention on track, the design included some 'lifelines,' where one could only veer off just so far before a lifeline would be thrown. In Earth terms, this is often understood as catalyst, and even more often experienced as big life changes that invite one to give up their old self and life, known as a 'dark night of the soul.'

If they Remembered their potential as a Creator Being, they had the ability to set in motion a series of changes both in their DNA, and ultimately, in their destiny. They would be able to rewrite their contracts, clear their karma and lay out a whole new timeline. This was something that had rarely been done, yet with the rise in consciousness that would be happening on Earth, it was not too far out to see this potential play out.

The desire for Oneness would be seeded in each fractal and create such a magnetic pull to the other aspects that it would be hard to resist, especially the more they woke up to their true nature beyond their human suits. Oneness was their truth. One can hide from truth, but never fully run away from it. The more we do, the more we'll be catapulted back at a faster pace.

All of Creation was eager for this new experiment, as they would be faced with an enormous mission, since Earth at this time-space was known for its very dense consciousness, as well as very individualistic and independent life journeys. But that was exactly what created the most potent contrast for them to move from an individual way of operating to entering a new era as a collective. All aspects of the Six-Crystal inserted a great deal of separation wounds into their lifetime, so each heart would be pulled to Remember the Oneness and Unity they are. This is the contrast and duality that wants to be experienced.

Their meeting points were carefully placed among their timelines, not just with each other in human form, but also with other multidimensional aspects of themselves. After all, they were meant to realise and embody the Oneness with All they are, thus All of Life and all of their multidimensional existence.

Each aspect would have certain experiences and gain specific wisdom, virtues and insights, that by the time they would all meet and come together, there would be an abundant exchange of codes and information that would be uploaded through their whole Being as One. Their individual wisdom would become collective wisdom. Any residual trauma, wounds or distortions would be faced by the love of All and dissolve with much more ease.

Their journey would be one of co-creation, rather than simply healing old karma, a journey that many had still chosen to complete on Earth.

Even humanity understood that the Age of Aquarius was inviting a more collective way of being, so it was no surprise to All of Creation what was to come.

Only the Six would spend the first decades of their lifetime in denial of their design and of their true destiny, until the activation sequences were set in motion, and all played out exactly as it was designed.

KEY CODE: A GREATER DESIGN

23. JUST A CRAZY DREAM?

Robbie heard Ana racing down the stairs, making a lot of noise.

"I had such a crazy dream!" She stormed into the kitchen where Robbie was sipping his morning coffee. He looked up, delighted by her beauty and curious about what she had to tell him today.

"Robbie, I had such a lucid dream, and I remember all of it. When I woke up, I had to pinch myself to see if I was still dreaming, because the dream … it felt so real, but not realistic," she said, while walking back and forth next to the table. Abruptly, she stopped to look him straight in the eye, "And I just gotta tell you!"

"I'm all ears, my Love."

"So, here it goes," she cleared her throat, wondering where to start.

"I Remember that we are a part of this meticulous, perfect, divine design. It blows my mind! And it has created this perfect orchestration of our lives, has brought us together, and it's going to bring all six of us together as we explore, experience and learn more about Oneness, about Unity. Six Beings, fully embodied as a soul cluster — and we are two of the six."

Robbie watched her and felt she had the energy of an excited puppy, mixed with a hint of confusion.

"There is no coincidence, at all. I could see the whole design, when we were born and where we were born — and I could see this Six-Crystal split into six different mini-versions of itself that then became their own unique forms, and even though we are different, we're also kinda the same. And it's like this geometric form — like, it split, and then it became … us." Ana frowned as she tried to explain the download she had received. She understood it with every cell of her Being, but translating it into words was a different thing.

"And I was seeing and understanding it all, but not as Ana — like I was seeing myself as one of the Six. It's like I had become the Six-Crystal itself. And I could understand everything about our life and what we're here for."

"Like, how fucking crazy is that?" She shook her head, overcome by surprise and disbelief.

Finally, Ana paused and looked at Robbie. He just looked straight back at her, another timeless moment of Oneness as their eyes connected. His only response was, "I Remember," as a tear fell down his cheek.

KEY CODE: DOWNLOAD

24. AUSTRALIA CALLS

Tiny felt refreshed after her nightly conversation with her higher self. She went back into town to a local bar and opened her email as she sipped a fresh mint tea. Delighted, she discovered that her WWOOF request had been approved. Months ago, before she even came to Egypt, she had applied to volunteer at an organic farm in Australia, and they had finally gotten back to her.

> Miss T. Yang,
>
> We are sorry for the delay, but we have had a very busy season here at The Haven and your email got misplaced. If you are still interested, we would like to inform you that we do have one spot open for an extra volunteer at our organic farm and you can start anytime in the next week. We understand if you may need some time to make life arrangements, but we do hope to hear back from you soon to know if you still want to join us!
>
> Kind regards,
> Miguel

"Arrange my life? I am ready!" she thought, already imagining herself on the next plane to Australia.

She didn't care about the twenty-hour-plus journey, or the jetlag that would kick in, all she could think about was the next adventure that had just opened up and that clearly made her heart beat faster.

"I guess this is what my higher self means by following my heart. This is loud and clear. This lights up my whole Being, like a zing-ding-ding throughout my body."

Her excitement overshadowed her doubts and fears of going to another foreign land. And in no time, Tiny was ready to leave this chapter in Egypt behind and start anew in the land of kangaroos and song lines.

KEY CODE: BREADCRUMB TRAIL OF EXCITEMENT

25. CONTACT

Now that Ana was aware of the Six-Crystal, she was eager to connect to the others. She couldn't wait to meet them, be with them, live with them, co-create with them and ... experience unity.

The Oneness she at times felt with Robbie was beyond words. Yet, he was her partner and lover, so it made sense to feel that close. She didn't understand yet how it would be to feel that Oneness with other people.

She had no interest in being polyamorous or being part of an orgy or anything like that, so her mind was boggled by what unity would look like with six people. Robbie and Ana had watched *Sense8*, a popular series on Netflix that introduced the concept of a cluster, where eight Beings emotionally, mentally and sensually are linked and are able to communicate and exchange abilities from across the world. Even though it revealed some future possibilities of a telepathic connection, to Ana it felt like the show was more about exchanging superpowers and randomly having sex together, than truly about embodying unity. But then again, she had no clue yet what unity would look or feel like.

"My life story will tell. Hopefully, by the end of my life, I will know."

She wanted to communicate with the others. Given she didn't know them yet, she had her mind set on opening up a telepathic line of communication with them. She believed that was bound to happen to them in the future anyways, so why not start now?

Every night before bed, she would send out a signal across space and time to the four others of the Six-Crystal, as she had no clue where they were. She created her own invocations to open contact:

> *I call upon the Six-Crystal.*
> *I call upon the Six-Crystal in my heart and connect all aspects back into One.*
> *I Know that All are Here Right Now.*
>
> *I am connecting my heart to yours and amplifying the Light grid that we create together.*
> *I see it done.*

The words would alternate:

> *I activate all aspects of the Six-Crystal Now.*
> *May every aspect wake up and Remember their collective nature.*
> *I connect to you Now. Respond with a sign. Over and out.*

Even when she asked for a sign, she didn't know what to expect, but at least she had fun while doing it.

Every evocation rippled out across the Light grid. Just like paving a neural pathway in the brain, the repetition started paving a stronger path between the sender and receivers, even though the others, in their human form, were not conscious of it yet.

KEY CODE: LIGHT GRID

26. WHAT IS ONENESS?!

"I have to Remember what Oneness is truly like. I need to know what unity consciousness is. We're all saying these words 'we are One,' but what is it actually like, Robbie?" Ana asked.

"I have a vague memory of what it's like," she continued, "in a reality where it literally felt like we were One, instead of being in these separate bodies. So, I need to know — how do we get to *be One* while I'm in this woman's body and you are this handsome man? How do we live as One? Move as One? I can't just speak these words out loud but internally believe myself to be a separate somebody. Oneness is Oneness. There are no two. But my mind can't grasp it when I'm over here and you're over there. That makes two."

"I know, my Love, the greatest paradox, huh. Wouldn't you agree this is part of the mission? What you just said is exactly what we are here to learn, experience and Remember," Robbie attempted to reassure her.

"Yeah. I do agree. I don't know if there is anything that holds my fascination more than this question. I could die for it. Yeah, that's exactly what I'm living for right now. I am here for it … but I have no clue how, babe." Ana couldn't help but add a touch of drama as she made her typical pout.

"Well, I guess given that you are here, and I am here too, we'll figure it out together, shall we?" Robbie smiled.

"Yes, team!" Ana declared with conviction as they sealed the deal with a kiss.

KEY CODE: ONENESS

27. THE SIX-CRYSTAL ACTIVATION

If Ana had asked Robbie to join her a few years ago, he would have thought she was bonkers. But after his glimpse of heaven, his communication line to the Divine was open and both Ana and Robbie were now invested in the activation of the Six-Crystal. For forty days, they engaged in an Activation Ritual to connect to the design and manifest it into their external reality.

Every morning, they sat cross-legged across from each other on the floor of their living room, yet internally, they imagined sitting in a circle of six and connecting to all aspects of the Six-Crystal.

They had created a sequence that they followed step by step:

Anchor into Self
Dropping into the heart.

Anchor into the Earth
Connecting into the crystalline core of the Earth.

Anchor into Source
Connecting to the core of the Universe and beyond, into Source.

Connect Two
Envisioning a thread of Light between each other's hearts, then allowing the energy to weave as an 8, the symbol of infinity.

Connect Triads
Imagining two triangles, one starting from Ana, one from Robbie, connecting to the four other imagined Beings sitting next to Robbie and Ana.

Close the Circle
Seeing a circle of Light that moves in a clockwise direction and connects all the dots.

As their devotion grew, more energy and more Light would surge within and throughout the Six-Crystal. The one imagined in their living room, the one in their own hearts, the four other crystals in the hearts of their soul cluster, and in all aspects across space and time.

As their energy field amplified, both started *seeing* more, as if they could read between the lines, listen to what was spoken in the silence and feel what was brewing under the surface. They needed less words, had little discussion, and moved into greater resonance with each other.

Even though their relationship became more harmonious, it didn't lose its juiciness. On the contrary, their polarity grew even stronger, and sex became not just lovemaking, but more like a Cosmic Affair that touched them in the depths of their Being. Letting their bodies be intertwined was the closest they could get, at least physically, to becoming One Body. More and more, the mind would be out of their way and their bodies would melt into One, being so engaged in the sexual flow that neither could discern where his or her body began or ended. Instead of speeding up, their body dance would slow down, making them more present with every movement and with the electric surges of energy it evoked in them.

And even when they physically sat across from each other in a room, they could feel one another. Robbie could predict when Ana got home from work exactly thirty seconds before she opened the door, and miraculously, their dream state started linking up. They now made fun of it, staying in bed in the morning and sharing their dreams, to find out that more often than not they had shared the same adventures together, unless one of them was healing or processing a past experience. Those remained individual dreams, although the other one would often show up and stand by as a loving beacon of support.

Two were becoming One. One Body. One Mind. One Heart.

KEY CODE: ACTIVATION SEQUENCE

28. THE TOO MUCH GIRL

Ana was a flamboyant kid.

"Ana, don't be so loud!" they told her when she cried out with laughter.

"Ana, be careful, you're gonna hurt yourself," they said as she courageously lifted herself into a tree that, yeah, might have been a bit too tall for her age.

"Ana, go to sleep!" they said as she stood on her bed after bedtime, singing out loud, using her hairbrush as a microphone.

"Ana, raise your hand if you want to speak!"

"Ana, stop talking to your classmate!"

"Ana, you're going to be sent out of class if you keep on talking!" they said at school.

Ana was the 'too much' girl. Too loud. Too hysterical. Too emotional. Too dramatic. Too sensitive. But also too funny, too cute, too beautiful if you would have asked her. She had a natural confidence and she wasn't easy to sway. When Ana had made up her mind, well, she had made up her mind and you better accept that as a fact. Negotiation was not her strength. But Ana's 'too-muchness' was just a cover up.

One day, when she was little, she proudly skipped towards her father to show a drawing she had made of him playing with Fergus, their one-year-old golden retriever.

"Daddy, Daddy, I made something for you!" she exclaimed, filled with pride. But she had interrupted his holy hour. He was watching football, and she had apparently entered the living room at a crucial point in the game.

"Not now, Ana!" he abruptly lashed out, waving her away with his hand. Quietly she drifted off, ran upstairs to her room, crumpled the drawing and fell on her bed in tears.

This wasn't the only time her dad had no time for her. It was just the first memory she could recall. He was a busy man, always worried about money, needing to work hard, and being at home was supposed to bring some much-needed relief from the stress at work. Having children who made lots of noise was not ideal for his mood.

Ana so longed for his attention. For his love. For his approval. She wanted him to be proud. She wanted him to tell her how good and smart she was.

When she was little, he would take her on his lap and tickle her, or he would move his leg up and down to 'ride like a horse' while she squealed with joy. In those moments she felt loved, but they would be short-lived, as after a while, she would have to get off his lap and leave him alone again.

She drank in those moments as if she had been deprived of water for a while, but the older she grew, the less often those moments would happen. She wouldn't sit on his lap anymore, yet the internal craving for his love found other loopholes.

The less attention he paid to her, the louder she became. If he didn't notice her when she walked up to him, maybe he would when she screamed for his attention. Everything she did, most of her 'too-muchness,' was fuelled by the unmet needs of her inner little girl, who just wanted to be loved by Daddy.

Her childhood had not been traumatic, yet somehow, this feeling of not being recognized and loved by her father had left a zinging pain in her heart. She had covered it up with her loudness, but deep within, her little girl was aching quietly in the corners of her psyche.

Ana looked back at her childhood and saw how this had played out in her relationship with Robbie. Before the accident, it was as if, subconsciously, she was expecting Robbie to give her the love and attention she craved from her father. She would get really loud and dramatic if she didn't get what she wanted from Robbie and made sure to get his attention if she needed it, even when he was in the middle of something. She wouldn't let him repeat how her daddy had ignored her. But of course, in return, her insatiable need for his attention had caused Robbie to ignore her at times, to not be as present with her as he could, and to just 'nod, smile and give short answers' to her ever-unfolding dramatic life updates. He wasn't showing up as his best version, but he got tired of her not giving him any space to breathe.

But now, they had become different versions of themselves. Life had given them a second chance, and she was willing to rewire those old dynamics.

Ana wasn't with Robbie to have a 'nice' relationship — she aimed for True Love. Finally, she could see how her unmet needs were not helping. Her pain didn't let her act from love, and it didn't evoke the most compassionate version of Robbie. Somehow, the dynamic would just repeat itself. Now that she was aware of it, it was up to her to do something about it.

It was time to heal her inner child. Those words sounded so big, but it was actually a lot simpler than she thought. Ana was good at talking, so it wasn't that hard for her to talk to her inner child. She was also visual, so she could easily imagine little Ana, her hair in two braids, crying quietly in the corner, feeling hurt and lonely. She would find out what little Ana needed, and through this practice, she would become more efficient at giving her adult self more love.

Self-love became not just a concept, but an actual experience. Ana genuinely started to love herself more, understand what she needed as a woman, and how she could spend time with her own inner little girl to guide her through this world and heal her wounds.

Ana was fascinated by the power of imagination and visualisation and the inner work that helped her see through this dynamic. Little Ana became a cheerful little girl again, playing and singing freely in her inner landscape, knowing that Daddy was a busy man, while feeling his love for her in his heart.

More and more, Ana's inner child found her way back to ease. Even though her father might have not given her the attention and love she wanted, Ana's nurturing attention and listening ear, simply her Presence coming from her adult self to her younger self, was like a healing balm to the wound she had felt as a child.

And as a result, this brought her closer to Robbie, as she was less expectant and demanding of him to take care of all her needs. She would ask for support when she needed it, and she would give Robbie the space to be alone when he wanted it.

Her cover-up was slowly being dismantled ... and she no longer needed to scream for what she wanted.

KEY CODE: INNER CHILD HEALING

29. TOUGHEN UP, BOY!

Little Robert was looking up at the playground castle where the other kids were playing and laughing. He watched some boys bravely running up and down the walkway and climbing up to the top. He looked a little startled. He didn't feel that brave — he felt scared and uncomfortable. But he was a boy. He had to be strong.

His mum would always give him a little push in the back when he hesitated, whether to go see Santa Claus or look up close at the animals in the zoo.

"Come on Robbie, don't be a freakin' pussy!" she would say, or, "I know your daddy didn't give you the balls to be a real man, but you're gonna have to toughen up!"

He would rather have just sat under a nearby tree and watched the other kids play. He liked being an observer; it made him feel at peace. But he had learned that it was not okay to just stand on the sidelines. He was looking at the other boys to see what was expected of him, so when his friend Matteo came up to him and asked, with red puffy cheeks, "Let's climb up to the castle, Robbie!" he followed, gathering all his courage to conquer the castle.

Arriving in the tower at the top of the castle, he realised it wasn't too bad to climb up there. But looking down, it was the climb down that terrified him even more. The height for little Robbie, with his fifty-two inches, seemed way too much.

It was only when Robbie became a teenager that he really toughened up. Before that, he always had more of a sensitive nature.

He was a dreamer who wrote love letters to the girls he fell in love with. He could stare at the ants in the grass for hours and observe what they were doing with their ant life. He remained quiet when his classmates made fun of others, and didn't bully in order to get attention or win popularity.

He was a sweetheart, yet at times, socially awkward with the girls. Since his love letters didn't have the effect he hoped for as a kid, he stopped caring and expressing his love for girls and had somehow concluded he would wait until he was an adult before making another attempt. He didn't have the looks, nor the muscles or the macho charm to win the girls, so he may as well just be okay with being single. And he was, quietly at peace with himself and losing himself in reading books.

*

Robbie was fifteen when his father died. Life turned around fast and little Robbie became a man too soon.

He started skipping school to smoke joints at the graveyard and was determined to rebel against life. Life was fucked up. He no longer believed there was a God, and if there was, then God clearly seemed against him — turning his life into misery before he even got the chance to fully live it. He didn't understand why his father was taken from him — he didn't deserve to be punished. He had been a good kid. He had been standing on the sidelines, but not anymore.

One of his first acts of rebellion was getting a piercing, a little ring in his left ear. And even though that's what the cool kids seemed to do, in his proper catholic neighbourhood, having a piercing or tattoo almost seemed as bad as blasphemy.

He enjoyed pushing people's buttons. He liked to offend. It was his way of finding an outlet for his own pain. Somehow, he wanted to make others feel some of the pain that he had, and yet, the devastation in his heart could never be made right by his frivolous acts.

His mother was his unwilling victim, receiving his unfelt grief and rage storms, while at the same time he felt responsible for her. That's why he started working in the nearby garage most weekends and evenings to make some extra money, as his mum didn't earn much as a cashier at the local grocery store.

His act lasted a few years, until the rebel started calming down and he focused more on work. Making money became his driver as he wanted to buy himself a Chevrolet.

Ana created a plot twist in his life. The freckles on her nose, her curly red hair, her green eyes and those long legs — he fell head over heels for her. She gave him back some life, another reason to live. Naturally, she broke down some of the armour he had built around his heart.

Their relationship consisted mostly of hanging out on Fridays at the park, partying late, then staying in bed most of the day on Saturdays, watching movies, having pizza nights and having the best sex ever. At least, that's what he told himself. Even though she was his first girlfriend, he was pretty sure what they had was pretty unique, compared with the stories of his buddies, filled with porn and short quickies.

When Ana and he had sex, it was as if she adored his body as much as he did hers. They would enjoy a passionate quickie, yet they could spend many hours on the weekend just lying in bed, staring at each other's sleepy faces and making out as long as they wanted to. It was probably his favourite way of spending the weekend, and the most restful break from his full-time job at the garage.

Even so, Robbie's anger over his father's death lingered and squashed down his joy for life. He still held resentment against life itself and he didn't have much excitement for his future. What was left in store for him? Working his ass off until he retired?

He hoped to have Ana by his side as long as possible. She was the sunshine in his life, and yet he wanted to hold off on living together, as having her too close only reminded him of the fact that one day she would leave. Either she would literally leave him, or she would die. Either way, his heart would shatter once again. It didn't even cross his mind that he might ever want to leave her. The future seemed gloomy. Not only would he lose Ana, but also his mum. It was a fact that there was more despair in the future. He couldn't come to peace with this and numbed himself to that harsh reality by having a few beers after work, and on Fridays, forgetting about life even more by getting wasted — without throwing up, that was the goal.

But as life sent a plot twist, it would only be the little ring in his ear that would leave a trace of his rebellious years.

KEY CODE: A GUARDED HEART

30. THE MEMORY OF DIVINE UNION

Tiny had been busy working at the Haven for a few weeks and needed a break to enjoy some peace and quiet. Together with some other WWOOF volunteers, she went on a camping trip to visit Uluru, Australia's most sacred mountain, also seen as the solar plexus chakra of the Earth.

She had decided to get up early in the morning, go see the sunrise by herself and be in awe of the majesty of the giant red rock of Uluru. She sat down and leaned against a tree, awaiting the first rays of sunlight to break through the night. She closed her eyes and connected to her heart, feeling gratitude for this new day, then intentionally opened her third eye to move into a trance meditation, completely unaware of what she was getting herself into.

Out of the blue, she started crying out loud. An incredible grief overpowered her. She couldn't yet understand why, but she just couldn't stop sobbing. Little by little, her mind caught up with what had been activated in the emotional body.

Tiny had never had a boyfriend. Being around her brothers, who teased her all the time, hadn't made her like boys much. As a teenager, she was way too shy to even speak to a male creature, and by the time she left college she was more into going on an adventure than finding a boyfriend.

As she travelled and came across so many new people and other travellers, Tiny had finally started to appreciate the men she met.

Occasionally, there was one who made her heart beat faster, and even made her blush, but she didn't have the courage yet to open up and make a move, so instead she shied away.

Yet, deep within, she was a true romantic. Hopelessly moved by Disney movies and romantic comedies, she still held the belief that there was one man who would one day steal her heart. He didn't have to arrive on a white horse, but he had to love her for exactly who she was.

The cry that escaped her mouth was almost like a heartbreak, even though her heart had never been broken. She felt the ache of missing her Lover, even though she had no clue who he was.

A vague memory started arising of a love affair so epic, even beyond the best Disney movies she had seen, that she kept trembling and shaking in tears.

> *Her heart started to Remember this Love.*
> *Her heart started to Remember her male counterpart.*
> *She Remembered the Union she once felt.*
> *The Sacred Marriage.*
> *The Divine Union she was a part of.*
>
> *He was everything she was, yet opposite,*
> *compatible and meeting her in all ways.*
> *He was the Yang to her Yin,*
> *and his Yin was met by her Yang.*
> *Together, One whole — One Being — One Love greater*
> *than anything else ever known.*
> *They knew how to weave their Essences together and*
> *create new potentials birthed from their coexistence.*
> *They knew how to move as One, while being fully*
> *anchored in their unique expression.*

She had never known a love like this, yet her heart must have known when she watched those Disney movies that more was possible than the 'dry' love that existed between most couples she had witnessed growing up. She was familiar with the sterile type of love that was more like an agreement, a trade between families, and only for the lucky ones, accompanied by a beautiful companionship.

The memory of this Divine Union and the exponential love she felt cracked her heart open, creating the longing for reunion, for wholeness and for Oneness. There was no way she would ever forget this memory that had unlocked in her heart.

KEY CODE: DIVINE UNION

31. Homeache

"None of this is real!" Ana exclaimed in tears.

Robbie simply witnessed it all from his lounge chair, while she paced the room furiously, eyes ablaze, hair wildly swinging with each angry stomp.

"None of it! How could I even believe that there is a soul cluster, or that I could connect to someone I don't know on the other side of the globe? I've been a fool! I've been crazy! I don't understand! How could you have not stopped me?!"

Robbie just listened, while patiently and lovingly holding space for her. He knew whatever he would say right now would only add fuel to her fire, and he did not want to provoke it and have it erupt like a volcano of blame onto him. *"Just let the fire blaze,"* he thought to himself, *"allow the pain to come out and let the fire turn the pain into insight."* At least eventually it would, so he decided to just let it rip.

Her fury covered a deep pain and desperation. Deep within, she didn't know if she could live on without being together with her soul cluster. Could she bear all the suffering happening on Earth without the support, love and guidance from her soul family? Could she continue living alone instead of All-One?

The feeling of separation was tearing up her heart. The heartbreak of a lover disappeared into thin air compared to the devastation she felt when she imagined herself cut off from her soul family. She had started this war and division in her own mind, but to her, it felt real. Real AF.

She collapsed onto the ground, her fury becoming a deep cry. A loud wail came from deep within her womb as she felt the excruciating pain of being away from what felt like her true Home. Suddenly, a flood of feeling trapped in this dimension, in this life and in this body engulfed her.

"I either want to forget all of this and never think of it again, or I want to go *back*. I want to go Home. I want to be *together* — as One — with my soul family. I want to go back to where we lived in harmony, to where we only knew love. This life is so painful. I can't live like this. I don't *want* to live like this."

Memories of her Ancient Future lurked in the back of her mind, reminding her of what seemed like better times. Her heartache was a Soulache, the ache for a Home beyond this life. All that was needed was for it to be felt.

Robbie approached her, knelt on the ground and lifted her chin up so he could look her in the eyes as snot and tears blasted across her face.

"Sweety, I know you long for Home. It may not help you right now, but I am here with you. You won't like what I'm about to say next, but I'm gonna do it anyway, because I assume you'd rather have me speak my truth, yeah?"

With droopy eyes, she softly looked up and whispered, "Yes," with a pout.

"Home is Here. Home is in your heart," Robbie said softly as he placed his left hand on her chest. "Right Here. What hurts is believing you are away from Home. That Home is *not* Here, or that Earth cannot be or is not good enough to be your Home. You hurt because you fight the truth, that Home is Here, right Now, in your heart."

Every word he spoke entered Ana's heart like a gong, creating a rhythmic beat as she received his message like a morse code. She didn't want to hear the message and frowned, but simultaneously her heart softened.

"Home — that place you Remember, that time, that world, the energy — what a privilege for you to Remember while most are asleep. Wouldn't it be more depressing to know that mainstream life is all there is?" he paused to let the question sink in.

"Instead, you *know* where we come from and where we are going. Home is pulling your heartstrings. I don't think we need to deny this pain. I love how you allow your tears to come out." Ana hardly believed his words, as people always told her she was 'too much,' but his calmness and presence revealed he was speaking truthfully.

"What if we're curious about what is hurting within us?" Robbie asked. "What if you find out what keeps your fire going and what in this world you absolutely cannot stand? You see, the thing that infuriates you can also be the thing that lifts you up, that gives you passion and purpose to do something about it, to make Earth into the Heaven you Know it to be. Oh dear, I'm going off on a tangent …"

"No, continue," Ana responded adamantly, "I need to hear this, even if I don't want to."

"Well, ultimately, my Love, I believe we are here to realise that Heaven is already here, we don't even need to 'make it happen.' We just need to take the blinders off our eyes and see all our old beliefs that convince us the world is dark, asleep or like hell. And stop watching mainstream media, for God's sake. Go Quantum. See a different world and you'll receive a different world. And it seems like you wanna be living in Heaven, don't you?" Robbie said with a big smile, unexpectedly grabbing Ana by her side to pull her onto the ground as he hunched over her. Caught by surprise, she snapped out of her own made-up story.

"Well, Miss, I sure love to be in Heaven with you," he confessed and kissed her on the neck while she squealed and giggled, but nothing on her mind thought of begging him to stop.

KEY CODE: HOMEACHE

32. Home is Here

Later that night, before she went to bed, Ana sat in the twilight with just the light of a few beeswax candles, her diary on her lap, reflecting on her day. She closed her eyes and tuned into her heart. She still felt the remnants of the Homeache she had felt earlier that day.

She received flashes of Home. It wasn't that the visuals were clear, but she could just feel it. It simply *felt* like Home. An energy wave washed over her and filled her whole body with tingles.

Again, it created a longing — to escape, to leave this Earth life behind, to melt into this energy and dissolve into formlessness. But then she remembered Robbie's words, "Home is Here."

And like a little light globe went off, her heart skipped a beat and she squealed out loud, "Yes, it is HERE! I feel it. I gotta get out of my head and into my heart. I can't logically get this, but if I simply *feel*, it's as if I can feel it *now!* I can *feel* Home, right here, right now."

The painful longing alchemized into desire and into an ecstasy that permeated Ana's whole Being. She softly fell on her back, spread her arms and legs like a starfish and bathed in the delight of this Home feeling. Not as something 'out there,' but as something 'in Here.' Robbie's words finally landed.

KEY CODE: HOMECOMING

33. THE UNDERWATER TEMPLE

"Come with me,"
I hear her angelic voice
as I'm drifting away.

Ana decided to take an afternoon nap after a busy morning shift at the coffee bar. She was becoming more aware of when the Angelic Presence would visit her. Sometimes she was wide awake and conscious, but more often than not, they met in dream state, where Ana's mind wouldn't interfere and she was more receptive to the Angel's transmissions.

I am standing at the ocean,
a breeze through my hair.
I hear a seagull squawk as it flies by.
The sand feels warm under my feet.
The waves are rolling
and my breath syncs up with their rhythm.

Here I feel at Home.
As I step into the waves,
it feels like the water becomes one with my own body.

The ocean calls me,
invites me,
pulls me in
to go deeper.

I feel relaxed
as I walk further,
and as my head goes underwater,
I Remember I can still breathe underwater,
naturally.

It feels as if I can float,
so I continue to go
deeper and deeper,
down and down,
deeper and deeper into the ocean.

Fully surrounded by her deep, dark blue waters,
I swim deeper and deeper,
going down and down,
down and down,
towards the bottom of the ocean.

As I float down,
in the distance I see a
bright fluorescent light.
It draws me.
It calls me.
It's as if it sings to me.

*Magnetically,
I'm pulled towards it.
As I draw closer,
I see the contours
of an underwater Temple
on an oval-shaped plaza.
In the middle,
a giant crystal emanates a beautiful light,
just like a beacon of light,
that spreads out and surrounds the whole Temple complex
in a bubble of translucent green light.*

*I move closer and closer,
until I swim up
to the crystal.
I feel its light
penetrate my whole body.*

*For a moment,
it feels as if
my body itself is a
beacon of light too.*

*I am now
pulled into the Temple.*

*Effortlessly,
I'm floating towards it.
I go through the entrance
in between the gorgeous tall pillars.*

*They remind me of the pillars of a Greek Temple,
yet it seems as if these are
made of crystalline white light.*

*It feels as if I know this place.
I have been here before.*

*As I enter the Temple,
I notice another big crystal in the centre.
A big, green radiating one.*

*"Welcome to the Jade Temple."
The voice of an angel
pierces the moment.*

*But I don't flinch or try to see
where the sound is coming from
as I'm guided and pulled towards
a floating bed.*

*The Jade Crystal at the centre
is surrounded by giant egg-shaped bubbles.
Big Bubbles of Light
that naturally adjust to one's body posture,
where one can lay down or take a seat.*

*I simply float through the edge of the bubble
and lay my body down,
feeling as if I'm simultaneously floating
and being held by the most comfortable pillows,*

the best waterbed ever.

I relax,
and feel held.

My whole body
is being Charged and Recharged
by Jade Energy.

I feel Nourished
and Nurtured.

I feel Safe
and Relaxed.

I am Resting and Restoring,
Rejuvenating and Replenishing
Right Now.

As time is timeless here,
I can be here for five minutes or an hour.
As I relax,
my body instantaneously restores itself.

*When I feel complete,
I see myself rise from the bed,
leaving the Giant Egg.
And as I do,
it feels as if I'm leaving
a giant shower of Jade energy.*

*Effortlessly and naturally,
gracefully and easily,
I leave the Temple
and float back.*

*I make my way back up,
swimming,
higher and higher,
coming all the way back
from the bottom of the ocean,
all the way back
to the beach where I started.*

*And as my feet start to touch the bottom again,
I walk out of the ocean
brand new.*

*And I know
that I can always return
to the Jade Temple
to Re-Source and Nourish myself.*

Only a few minutes later, Ana woke up fully energised.

"Wow, I haven't had such a good nap in a looooong time." She looked outside her bedroom window and pondered. *"Whoa, that underwater temple felt so real, and so known. Mmm, I wonder if it was just a dream? But I sure want to go back there."*

KEY CODE: THE JADE TEMPLE

34. Meeting Yu-Ka-Na

As often as she could, Tiny got up early in the morning to catch the sunrise before she started her morning shift at the Haven. She would drive to Cape Byron Beach to greet the sun, set intentions for the day, sometimes do some yoga, and always end with a meditation. And if it was her lucky day, she would spot some whales from the lookout point at Cape Byron Lighthouse.

On a cool summer morning, she was deep in meditation when he appeared. He felt so familiar. It was as if she was looking at herself, but in another form — recognizing herself in this male body.

"I am Yu-Ka-Na."

His every consonant was pronounced with extra emphasis and with a deeper, guttural sound.

"I am from Andromeda."

The communication line seemed very thin, as if the words being transmitted were only for her conscious mind to connect to. Simultaneously, streams of information entered her subconscious, making her heart feel all the feels and evoking Remembrances of another dimension and a star planet that would let so many pieces fall into place.

This meeting point unlocked a memory within her from a galactic timeline. She started to Remember herself as a Being on Andromeda.

They both had a light blue skin tone, long light hair covering their shoulders and wide eyes that reflected the cosmos.

This is where she knew Divine Union from. She could immediately feel the interconnectedness with his Being. As he stood in front of her, she was aware of the illusion it created as she felt her Being intertwine with his. Two aspects of the same coin, Yin and Yang — complimentary in every way. They had been in this constellation on Andromeda for many light years, which would be multiple lifetimes on Earth. A Union that could not be broken, there was only Oneness. Nothing like arguing, sacrificing or compromising existed there. One's highest good was the highest good of both. Nothing had to be denied. All was included and already embraced. All decisions were made in the highest good of both and of the wider community. They were creatures of love and lived in a higher density.

Life on Andromeda was oh so dear to Tiny, especially because her counterpart was there. She didn't want to use the name twin flame, as those connections often carried lots of karmic burden, so she had learned, but this Union consisted of pure Love, Harmony and Oneness.

Humanity had no idea yet how to love this way, yet her heart Remembered and had longed for it. It was probably this she had been seeking, and him she had been longing for her whole lifetime.

With him next to her, she felt an undeniable wholeness. Completion. She had no other words to describe it. She knew her spiritual teachers would say she had to be One within herself, but she didn't know for sure if they knew what Divine Union was, or if they had ever experienced it. How could you be whole, when a part of you is literally in another dimension? When half of you is in another time and space and you can't reach out? It was a mystery she couldn't solve yet.

After that first meeting, for the first few nights, Tiny cried herself to sleep as the memory of this love had blasted her heart open. Often, upon waking, she could feel Yu-Ka-Na. He would enter her field and she would know instantly, feeling the sense of reunion and wholeness again.

"How? What am I supposed to do? How am I supposed to deal with this? I can't understand why I am so far away from the love of my life. I mean, my love within the cosmos, the love of my existence?" A tinge of despair came through her question.

"I am Yu-Ka-Na. It is in the Oneness that we find each other. I too have grieved, when you left our home planet and answered a calling to go to Earth. Yet, we knew this was our next level of Remembering our Oneness — as truly we cannot be divided, separate or away from one another."

Tiny received his words in a dreamlike way. It was hard to tell if she was imagining it or not.

Yu-Ka-Na continued, "I have followed every step on your journey, and it has taken me many Earth years to connect with you in this way, yet, never did I stray too far from your side. Similarly, at all times, I can feel your presence here, watching over me, as if you're caressing my head. It is only when we hold on to a previous form of exchange, of beingness and togetherness, that we cause ourselves to hurt. I am Here with you Now, to evoke this Remembrance so you too can experience the Oneness that always is and has been, and that will never fade."

Oneness. She knew she was One with Yu-Ka-Na on Andromeda, but her mind couldn't grasp or go beyond the experience that he was there, and she was here, apart and separate from each other — the exact opposite of the Oneness she had once known and that now tasted like a bittersweet memory.

KEY CODE: GALACTIC REUNION

35. FROM CRAZY TO GENIUS

Robbie sat at the kitchen table, his head bowed down. Ana had not often seen him in tears. He was a gentle teddy bear, yet also 'the tough guy' and wouldn't show his emotions that easily.

"What's up, babe? Everything okay?" Ana asked as she pulled up a chair to sit next to him.

"Yeah, it's just, I'm letting it all out, riding the emotional wave. You know how it goes," Robbie said with a soft smile, tears running down his face.

"Mmmm, babe."

"I'm not even sure if I ever told you, but now I'm just ..." he tried to find his next set of words amidst the grief that wanted to pour out. "I'm just healing the relationship with my dad, I think. It's beautiful. I'm just releasing all this grief in my heart." He sobbed a little more before speaking again.

"You know my father died, right? He committed suicide when I was fifteen. It's something that taints you, you know. Not only do you lose a parent, but the way it happened — it just struck me like lightning. And I was so angry at him! I was so fucking angry. I turned into one hell of a teenager and gave my mum a hard time, even though he was the one I was angry at. She didn't deserve my rage and my stubbornness, but I just couldn't get over the fact of his selfish act to leave us. And we hadn't seen it coming, at all. It was just a shock to our whole family." Robbie exhaled deeply, as he simultaneously let go of the emotional charge.

"So, 'angry Robbie,' that's how most people knew me. I truly believe that falling in love with you, Ana, brought more softness to my heart. It made me see that life was still worth living and that I could have fun again. Maybe a little too much fun and drinks, but hey, that changed, didn't it," he poked her with a sarcastic smile.

"Right now, I'm just starting to see things from a different perspective, and it blows my heart wide open. I was connecting into my higher self and witnessing what happened from a soul level. I was seeing and understanding it as a catalyst and what it was for."

He paused for a moment, then continued, "Taking responsibility and owning that I too have wanted this and agreed upon this before my birth. I know so many people have a hard time with this, especially when it comes to the most traumatic events in our life, but Ana, it's so clear to me — when I face the truth, I can *see* it, I can *sense* it, and I can *own* it. This is the life circumstance I wanted to have, and my dad played a great role in it. It makes me grateful for his soul to have played his part, because that ain't an easy life path either!"

Robbie looked up, directly into Ana's eyes. "I saw my father as the bad guy, as the most selfish man I've ever known. And now, I am seeing a whole different version of him."

"My father was a Genius," his voice trembled. "It's the first time I am saying this, and it's the truth. It's painful, but liberating and beautiful at the same time to be reconciling this. He had a brilliant mind. He had a doctorate degree at university, had written a progressive PHD, and was working on innovative research at Princeton University. I mean, as a kid, I was fascinated by how he would teach me about the cosmos and physics. He would get so caught up in it he would forget I was just a kid, 'cause I couldn't keep up with all the equations and stuff he was talking about." He shook his head.

"The way he saw the universe — I think he understood the multidimensionality of this reality, that he could see patterns and geometries and truly see beyond what most people can see. His mind worked like a giant orchestration, like a radar network that operated at such a high speed. But it also made him confused, otherworldly almost, and not able to truly relate, like he lived with his head up in the clouds."

"I believe he had a brilliant mind and had so much genius in him, but there is only a fine line with insanity. I think his intelligence literally might have driven him crazy inside. I can imagine now that life was just too much to handle for him, but underneath all of that, I now see his genius, Ana. My father was a Genius!"

"Love, I didn't know. I don't know what to say. This is deep stuff." Ana was left speechless.

"The best part is, I got to see what this is leading me into. I'm feeling it, how this is related to my own passion and purpose, to my own destiny," his energy started rising and his excitement bubbled up.

"Whoa, tell me about it!" Ana eagerly responded.

"I've always had a heart for the weirdos, the outcasts, the outsiders. I've always naturally gravitated towards them, the crazy ones and the misfits. Every class or school had at least one of them, well, more than one," he chuckled.

"Ana, it's the 'weird and crazy ones' who are the geniuses of our world, yet up until now, they've mostly been living on the sidelines. How often is it that only *after* someone's death do we start to recognize their unique genius? Think of Picasso, Einstein, or Tesla! They lived a life in seclusion and their mastery was rarely recognized. I can only imagine they each carried a deep sense of loneliness."

"That's what I want to change, Ana! If I look at our generation and at teenagers, these millennials and Gen Z, babe, they have fucking brilliance and genius in them! And it's the genius who is able to pioneer a new way. These geniuses are here to carve out new ways of being, of living and of operating in this world."

"The old's gonna burn in flames," even Robbie liked to add a titbit of drama as he was getting all excited, "and it's not the ones who are stuck in their boxes, listening to mainstream media or following the rules who are gonna create change. We gotta honour the weirdos and the crazy ones. They are different. They don't fit into this world. Just like us, they often feel like they don't even belong in this world. They are more connected to their multidimensional nature than anyone who's still playing life according to the rules."

Robbie got up from his chair. "Let's bring the crazy ones together, the coup of the century! Let the crazy ones take over!" They both burst out laughing as Robbie now stood on his chair, with one arm in the air as if he was a freedom fighter leading a revolution — a revolution of love, in this case.

"We're here for a whole new world, aren't we? That probably sounds crazy still to most people, but that's exactly my point, Ana. I don't know how it looks yet," he stepped down from his chair, "but I am envisioning something like an online platform for millennials who resonate with this. Damn, social media has been hard for our generation, igniting even more comparison, insecurity, and I believe more disconnect, but at the same time, it's the network through which we can find them and they can find us. I wanna bring the crazy ones together! I wanna hear their stories, know what they are dreaming of and the future they see, the things they are secretly working on and the spiritual gifts they've been hiding. I wanna know their understanding of the world, hear about their pain and loneliness, and I want them to know and feel that they are not alone. I don't want them to live in isolation anymore. I don't want them to have to hold their crazy geniusness by themselves. I believe if we do this together," he ended with a dramatic pause, "then no one has to take their own life anymore."

KEY CODE: GENIUS

36. LIGHT LANGUAGE ACTIVATION

A ka na a wa ka na
Da yang
Ga na she ho
Aya le ka nohwa
Ie ya ha na
Oya le you
Ang ka na y a
Eyo wa la ye ga na ra ya
Iiii o
Aaaa he
Ke no ma
An ga na go
Ya neya ho
Ha ya leee ga na ma yo

Tiny had been practising all kinds of sounding and toning with her voice. Lately, these weird sounds and vowels would come through. On a call with her mystery school guide, and now friend, Ayana, she told her about the sounds. Of course, Ayana asked her to share more about it.

"Yeah, well, I don't know if I can do it right now, as normally it happens when I'm really in the mood and feeling connected, you know."

"Oh, don't be shy, Tiny. Just give it a try. Just go for it. You wouldn't have told me this if you didn't want to share those sounds with me, because you already knew I would ask you this."

Tiny couldn't disagree with that.

"Okay, give me a moment." Tiny closed her eyes and took a deep breath. She made a big sigh and sounded like a horse, "Brrrrrr."

Another deep inhale, and then first, just a sound, her tone:

♪ *OOOOOOOOOOEEEEEEEEEEEEEEEEH*

It helped her to recalibrate and reconnect. Then after a few seconds, the flow just ripped:

Yo ka le ya no
Ang ka ho na da
Ie ya do ha la
Ya ke na ma ha

There was a rhythm to it and a cadence that had a tribal vibe.

Ye la ho ma ja
Ka wa ho me ya
Awa ya ka na ma he yo wa

"Something like this?" Tiny asked, with a shy smile as she lifted her shoulders.

"Aaaah, my dear! I already thought so," Ayana said, "you are starting to channel Light Language!"

"Light Language …" she had seen and read about it when she started finding all these #starseeds on social media, but it didn't cross her mind that these sounds could actually be Light Language. It just felt weird, and a little crazy. And it didn't make sense — for she had no clue what she was doing!

"I get it, dear," Ayana said when Tiny shared her concerns. "It's not about making sense. This is beyond the sensical, the logical or the rational. This goes beyond your mind," she said, pointing her finger to her head.

"You just let it rip! You just let it flow. It's not about what sense it needs to make. It's about letting the sounds, tones and vowels come through you — trusting the flow of it, trusting the divine, open receptive vessel that you are. It's sensing and knowing that your higher self and subconscious mind know exactly what is coming through."

She paused for a second.

"It wouldn't surprise me if you're going to start to bliss yourself out when doing this, because your sounds carry codes and frequencies that do stuff to your body, you know," Ayana widened her eyes to stress her words.

"Yeah, I feel that," Tiny responded, "I guess that's why I wanted to share it with you. I have been feeling insecure about it, but it's actually pretty cool. Like when I make my own tone, it just realigns and recalibrates my *whole* body."

"Yes, dear!" Ayana clapped her hands with excitement. "Our sound is one of the ways we plug into the universal matrix. Through sound and vibration all is and has been created. We have just forgotten our creation power that comes through sound. You are retrieving more and more pieces as you go. It's beautiful to witness!"

"You're hinting at the fact that there are more pieces?" Tiny asked.

"There are always more pieces, my dear! I believe you remember how in Ancient Egypt they believed we have 360 senses, right, reflected in the circle that has 360°. That is no coincidence, of course. So yes, there are many more pieces, and you at least have the rest of your lifetime to discover them," Ayana concluded with a big smile.

KEY CODE: LIGHT LANGUAGE

37. COMMUNICATION LINE

Weeks passed without any visible progress, yet Ana didn't give up. She was like a pit bull, determined to make a connection with the others of the Six-Crystal. They would have to show up one day, sooner or later, at least that's what she told herself.

One day, during their morning meditation, Robbie was sitting across from her as they tuned into the Six-Crystal. After a few minutes, Ana's focus got interrupted when she sensed a presence on her right. She peeked out of her eyes, but no one was there. She closed her eyes again and tuned in energetically.

She could feel her sitting next to her. Ana opened her right eye to peek again, half expecting to see someone in the room, but there was still only the cat laying on the windowsill.

Ana closed her eyes again. Her heartbeat rose, eager to see who was there. It literally felt as if there was another woman in the room. She couldn't see her with her physical eyes, so she dropped her attention into her heart and connected from there. As she continued breathing, she sensed her presence again.

She felt her energy. Slowly, she started seeing her features — it was definitely a woman. She seemed rather tiny or small, maybe even younger than Ana. As her features continued to become clearer, Ana imagined the woman having short, black hair. She couldn't see more details, but she connected more and more to this woman's energy.

The energy started to flow in an endless figure of eight between them: from Ana's heart to the woman's root, going up to the back of her heart and then flowing back from the woman's heart to Ana's root ... creating an infinity loop between them. Energy flowed in all directions, linking and syncing them up.

Again, Ana peeked out of her right eye to see if anyone was sitting there, as she couldn't tell the difference between what felt real or imagined.

"I guess that's a good sign," she thought, while also questioning the validity of this experience, yet she decided to just go with it.

After talking to an angel and getting her wings back, she was not easily surprised anymore. Even though this was all happening within the invisible realms, the first key of their unique activation sequence had been set in motion. This communication line was now fully opened.

KEY CODE: INFINITY LOOP

38. SIMULTANEITY

Tiny sat under the night sky near Uluru for another evening meditation. She had become used to transcendental and multidimensional experiences when visiting the mountain but would have doubted whether she was prepared for this next phase.

She had entered a deep theta state, opening the door to all dimensions. This time she didn't travel into other realms. She was fully present in her body, yet her awareness felt spacious and able to scan the edges of creation. She became no-body, in no-space, in no-time. She was no-where.

Suddenly, she started sensing a presence near her. It felt different than Yu-Ka-Na. It was as if it was sitting right next to her, to her left, yet she knew the only thing next to her was a giant red rock.

She continued breathing and emptying herself over and over again, yet the presence kept pulling her attention and bringing her back into the awareness of being in her body.

Her curiosity asked, "Who are you?"

Tiny never received much visual input, but she received more and more through sound and vibration, opening up her clairaudient abilities.

She picked up some syllables, "Ya-Na."

Ya-Na … it felt like the presence was a woman, not introverted like herself. She sensed a lot of red energy, a more fiery personality.

"Are you from Andromeda?" she continued.

No response. Just this came through, "Hu-Man."

"Mmm, human, just like me. That's why you feel so close."

"Are you dead?" she wondered.

"No."

Wait — a woman, human, next to me — but not dead.

"But you're not here?" Tiny's mind was boggled. She hadn't experienced something like this yet. "How?"

Her inner voice whispered, "Relax."

Meanwhile, Ana was sitting more than 8,000 miles across from her in meditation, simultaneously feeling Tiny's presence next to her. The communication line between them had opened up and the energy exchange had started.

With Ana's presence still next to her, Tiny entered another deep theta wave. She now started seeing geometric forms spinning and swirling around. It looked like a merkaba, at least from the six points she could distinguish. Yes, she could see two intersecting tetrahedra, spinning in opposite directions.

The giant form appeared in front of her, as if it appeared onto a large movie screen, then it moved closer towards her until it fully surrounded her, with Tiny sitting at the centre of it. Then, it fully collapsed into a zero-point, imploded, and expanded to the size of a ping pong ball that entered and settled into her heart.

Tiny felt it hit her chest as it moved into her heart space, as if something had truly entered the chambers of her heart. She swayed backwards a little, then centred herself again.

The Six-Crystal started glowing in her chest, unlocking the next key of her Remembrance. Tiny didn't realise yet what was happening, but nothing would ever be the same again.

KEY CODE: BILOCATION

39. DIVINE ORCHESTRATION

Ana told Robbie about the presence she had felt in the room during their meditation the other morning.

"Robbie, I'm gonna tell you another crazy thing. I know you're probably gonna tell me it ain't crazy, and I probably should be getting used to it, but yesterday morning, I swear I could feel a woman sitting next to me. I even peeked and opened my right eye to see if someone was there, even though I knew that couldn't be the case, and of course I only saw our kitty," Ana rattled like a whirlwind, "but *no!*" She took a deep breath to prepare herself for the next wave of words. "There was no one, and yet it felt as if she was as real as you sitting in front of me now, Robbie!"

"So, of course, I assumed she was part of the Six-Crystal, because I mean, that's what we've been trying to connect to for weeks. So, as I tuned into her and connected to her heart, I had a felt sense that she is this small, cute Asian woman. She looks young, maybe our age or younger, or maybe that's just a stereotype that Asian people never seem to age. And you know, Robbie, I don't like to speak in stereotypes, and yet," she continued raising her dramatic voice, "I have been conditioned by this very culture to think and assume these stupid things about people I don't even know, and I can't help it, so, anyway, back to my point — she is young, has pale skin and black hair. And that's all I know."

Suddenly, disappointment dawned on her because of the little information she actually had. What had seemed like a huge revelation now seemed to be just peanuts.

"This is, well, a first-timer, Ana, so don't be down for whatever your mind is telling you right now, honey. It's progress, right? You've been wanting this for so long, and now you're one step closer." Robbie's words soothed her, as always.

He was right. She did feel one step closer — to at least one of the Six-Crystal. She couldn't believe the patience she had to conjure up for this design to unfold 'in perfect timing' while she was ready to dance together in heaven, at least, that's what she thought.

A few weeks later, Ana got the intuitive hit to look up #crazyones on the Internet. Soon she landed on Instagram and started scrolling through the different posts with that hashtag. She was kinda bored, sometimes intrigued or even disgusted by what people were showing online. From happy dogs to drunk teenagers, full body tattoos, to some lame quotes and pictures that shocked with #toomuchinformation.

She continued scrolling until she saw a picture of an Asian girl holding up a text with symbols. She stopped and looked closer in disbelief. Could this be? Her heartbeat spiked to 150 bpm in a nanosecond as she tapped the picture to open the post.

Mysterious Symbols in Ancient Egypt. Secrets hidden everywhere, only to be uncovered for those who can read into the mystery.

Okay. This girl had a way of saying things. Ana checked her Instagram profile:

@themysterytraveller
Just like Moana, I set sail to discover the world and meanwhile ... myself.
#starseed #mysteryschool #intotheunknown

Ana chuckled. A Disney fan. The girl definitely looked younger, but Ana had mistaken Tiny's age by at least five years.

What were the chances — one in seven billion? There was no way Ana would have ever found Tiny if she had tried to look for her, but life's mysterious ways had worked their magic through Instagram's algorithm and made Tiny's picture appear on Ana's phone.

Ana had simply followed her gut feeling. She just wanted to look for the #crazyones after her talk with Robbie about genius — and found Tiny on her travel adventures in Egypt.

The chances are small, but not when you take divine orchestration into account — then you have 99% inevitability of your divine appointments happening in divine timing. And so, they did ...

Ana sent a DM to Tiny. Short and sweet, mysterious and direct.

Hi Moana Lover & Mystery Traveller,
I believe you showed up in my meditation, as if you were sitting next to me. If you don't believe that this is crazy, then I believe we need to talk!

Things were about to get real, Ana thought. Finally, she would soon find out if this Six-Crystal was a trick of her mind or not.

Only a week later, Tiny opened her message on Instagram. Working on the farm took up most of her time, and she was more engaged with real life than with *Fakebook* and *Instafamous*.

Ana's message came as a surprise, and no surprise, at the same time. She scrolled through Ana's profile — because that's how you size someone up these days, right — and appreciated her long, curly red hair. Ana definitely seemed more confident than her. She seemed more expressive, untamed and a little wild, like a tiger.

Tiny enjoyed life's mysteries and this message felt good to the spiritual seeker in her. Just like in *The Alchemist*, one of her favourite books, she loved it when life offered unexplainable treasures right on her doormat.

A few days later, Ana and Tiny had a video call on Telegram. As the call started, both were speechless as tears welled up in their eyes. It didn't make sense why they would be crying, but their meeting touched their hearts.

"I'm sorry, I don't know what to say. I normally always know what to say. I don't get why the first thing you need to see are my tears," Ana apologised, feeling a bit self-conscious.

"It's okay," Tiny responded in her soft voice. Feeling Ana's presence immediately reminded her of the fiery presence she had sensed during that meditation near Uluru.

She remembered Ana's message on Instagram, and only now fully realised the unbelievable fact that both had witnessed each other during their meditation. Whoa! Of course — the "Hu-Man" she felt was not dead — but she'd had no idea she would actually be meeting this woman.

After their tears dried up, Ana and Tiny talked for at least two hours. In the best way she could, Ana summarised what had happened over the last year: the car crash, Robbie's coma, how it changed her life, how she would have these surreal dream experiences, and lastly, the download of the Six-Crystal.

Ana knew it would sound crazy to any 'normal' person, yet Robbie seemed to Remember and she believed that Tiny was somehow a part of this design, so she had no choice but to share it all and wear her heart on her sleeve. Tiny just seemed to be listening, her dark eyes filled with curiosity, her head gently nodding once in a while.

In return, Tiny shared about her travel experiences and how she had opened up to the mystical and mysterious invisible realms, how in dream state she would journey across time and space, how she had met her divine union partner — her galactic counterpart — and had started to Remember her own multidimensional nature. Even though Ana's story was out of the ordinary, it didn't sound *more* crazy than her own recent experiences.

But more importantly, hearing about the Six-Crystal reminded Tiny of what happened during that one meditation. She shared with Ana that she too had felt a presence and had also received a geometric form that then anchored into her heart. She understood it was the Six-Crystal when Ana talked about it. Dots were connecting. Things that did not make sense started to make more sense. And yet, many more questions than answers were raised about how any of this was possible and what was next.

They both needed time to integrate. Not only had they exchanged words for two hours, but their meeting had also catalysed the next unlocking within their own Being, preparing them for what was to come next — their physical meeting. Little did they know how that would accelerate their life's mission.

KEY CODE: DIVINE APPOINTMENT

40. SIX SEES ALL

SiX witnesses it all. SiX sees how they crash, how they wake up, how they travel, how they Remember. Every moment of Remembrance creates a surge of energy in SiX's field.

> *Formless,*
> *yet ever-present,*
> *observing all that appears.*
> *Holding that same Desire*
> *to merge back into Unity,*
> *to let all that has been separate be magnetised back*
> *into the Remembrance of its completion and wholeness*
> *in all forms,*
> *across all time/space/dimensions.*

SiX holds this Knowing. It is literally the only thing it Knows, and simultaneously it witnesses the play that unfolds for all aspects across the Six-Crystal.

It is everywhere and nowhere. Sees All and doesn't experience time. It rests in its infinite nature, yet can reach into the depths of its own Being to see the veil it has put on, see how asleep it is, while the design is encoded at the core of each aspect.

Thus, Knowing that All in perfect timing will access the codes to Reactivate their Remembrance and Know they are One.

KEY CODE: SIMULTANEITY

41. WHITE BUTTERFLIES

"Have you seen the white butterfly?" Tiny asked.

"What do you mean?" Ana asked with a sense of astonishment.

"Did you receive the white butterfly I sent you?"

"The white butterfly you sent me — Tiny, what are you talking about?"

"Well, I was playing with this idea of sending you an animal, instead of just a message, you know, as part of opening up our telepathic connection. So, I sent you a white butterfly. Have you seen it somewhere in the last day?"

"Have I seen a white butterfly in the last day? Girl, I don't know what you have done, but I have seen white butterflies my whole life, especially since our car crash. That is now like, more than a year ago. I don't know which butterfly you sent me, but I have seen white butterflies show up at the most random places at the most random times. So yes, I have seen them. But, uhm, now you are telling me you sent me only one white butterfly, like, yesterday?"

"Yes, true!" Tiny answered diligently. "I sent it yesterday at 8:08 a.m. my time, which would be 1:08 p.m. your time. So, did you see one yesterday?"

"No, girl, I did not." Ana paused and pondered, "Robbie is talking about all this quantum stuff, how time does not exist, how there is only Now, and so, I'm just wondering if your game just fell flat, aka failed," she put it bluntly, while she simultaneously tried to figure out what was happening, "or maybe, your one butterfly multiplied and spread out across time. Or maybe you're still gonna send more butterflies to me and then they just end up in my past. I don't know. This stuff makes my head spin." She rolled her eyes. "What I want to say is thank you for sending me the white butterfly! Do you actually know the meaning of it?"

"No, I don't! But let's find out."

After their call, Ana reminisced about all the times she had noticed a white butterfly. The first time she remembered was when she must have been about seven years old. Her grandmother had just passed away and she was playing in the garden. She was sitting on the grass, staring at the bees buzzing around the flowers, as her mom walked up to her. A white butterfly passed by.

"Look! A butterfly!"

"Yes, that's Grannie saying hello," Mom said. "She is now in heaven, but when you see a white butterfly, you know she is around."

"Is Grannie now inside the white butterfly?" Ana asked, a little shocked.

"No, dear," Mom said gently, "as Grannie's body is no longer here, she just sends this white butterfly to visit us and say hello to us."

"Oh, hello Grannie!" Ana said. "Message received, over and out."

"Oh, wait, 'I love you Grannie!' Will you send this message back to Grannie, dear butterfly?" she asked, as she moved up close to the butterfly, making it fly away, high up in the sky. Ana believed the butterfly was now answering her request and taking her message to heaven. She waved to the sky with a big smile.

Ana smiled as she thought back, both about Grannie and that first white butterfly she remembered. She was sure they must have been around so many times, but the time of the car crash was definitely another moment where it stood out the most.

It didn't make sense how this butterfly just appeared right in front of the window as the car crashed down. How did she even notice it in that shocking moment? In the dark? And why was it there? It sure wasn't Grannie, so was it Tiny, or was it a sign? From whom, or what? From her own higher self — waving at her and letting her know, "Hey, I am here with you!"?

Since the crash, white butterflies had accompanied her on many walks. She had even wondered if suddenly, there were a bunch more butterflies out here, but even when she took a trip to Quebec in Canada, a white butterfly appeared on her first walk into the woods.

They would also show up as pictures or symbols, in ads, on social media, or on decoration. It must be a yellow cab thing — you see it more when you're looking for it, at least that's what she told herself.

Ana looked up the spiritual meaning of seeing a white butterfly. There were so many explanations on Google, so she followed her gut feeling to feel what stood out and felt true, creating her own explanation.

> When you see a white butterfly, it is like a message straight from the heavens. Know that you are not alone, and your spirit guides are watching over you.
> People often see white butterflies after the passing of a loved one, which can be seen as a gentle reminder that their soul lives on.
> Let the white butterfly bring you peace, comfort, and a heavenly warm embrace.

The true meaning of the white butterflies remained a mystery, but ultimately, it didn't matter if it was Tiny, an angel, or Ana's higher self who had sent these white butterflies. They simply reminded her that she was never alone, and she liked to believe it was a message from the other side of the world, or beyond.

KEY CODE: ANGEL SIGNS

42. INNER UNION

Tiny's relationship with Yu-Ka-Na had faded into the background. She was often aware of him, as if he was watching over her, and remembered when they had spent time together in dream time at night. Even so, the agonising pain of separation and the dimensional gap that would forever keep them apart, at least in her mind, had caused Tiny to close down her initial eagerness to connect with him.

Convinced she would never find a love like this again and therefore considered her love life to be non-existent, she dove into ancient teachings and mysteries to channel her energy, but her romantic nature could not be denied.

It was not until her telepathic communication line with Ana opened up that things started to shift. From the moment they met online, they didn't just speak through words — their communication channel opened at multiple levels simultaneously, with an exchange on the mental, emotional, energetic and soul levels. Each person's Essence held certain keys that unlocked a specific sequence in the other. This was all meticulously designed pre-birth, and now set in motion through this new meeting point. The young women, so eager and excited about their connection, could hardly grasp the vastness of what was actually happening between them.

And it was so that Tiny received the Inner Union Codes from Ana's field, through which she naturally moved into the reclaiming of her own Wholeness and Holiness, an inner reunion with all aspects of herself, the 360° of the circle that wanted to be held, loved and integrated.

As she restored the Inner Union within her own heart, feeling more and more fulfilled, whole and complete with each passing day, her connection to Yu-Ka-Na was ready for its next step. She was now able to Be in Re-Union with him across the dimensional gap. She started to experientially understand that the time-space distance was illusory in nature, as she could meet him in dream state or simply recall his energy through imagination.

He was Here with her Now.

Their connection amplified to the point where Tiny could not tell if it was made up or truly happening, but in her inner experience, she was united with Yu-Ka-Na, and thus united with Her-Self.

This Inner Union washed away the lingering remnants of the separation, the distance and the aloneness she had felt, and was replaced by the Oneness that always is, has been, and will never fade.

KEY CODE: INNER UNION

43. COMING HOME

It didn't take long before they all wanted to be together. It was clear for Tiny that her time at the farm was coming to an end, and just like last time, she was ready to pack up her bags, leave her life in Australia behind and move on to the next chapter — one that felt connected to her destiny.

She arrived at Sacramento Airport on the day of the Autumn Equinox and drove north, towards Mount Shasta. A few hours later, she arrived at Ana and Robbie's house in the woods. She was about to ring the doorbell, when her gaze was drawn to a flower box, where she saw a white butterfly fluttering around. "*Magic is here*," she smiled, taking a deep breath before she hit the bell.

Ana ran to the door and opened it wide with a big smile, full of excitement. "You're here! Welcome home!"

She embraced Tiny and squeezed her first, real close, then relaxed into a hug that neither seemed to want to let go of. Fireworks exploded in their hearts, while their bodies were as still as living statues. Again, tears welled up in their eyes, as if they had been waiting their whole lives for this moment.

Robbie slowly came down the hallway, allowing space for this precious moment to take as long as was needed. Finally, Ana let go of Tiny, who hadn't noticed Robbie standing behind her, as her eyes had been covered by Ana's red hair that smelled like coconut.

"Tiny," he said with his deep, warm voice, while gently opening his arms. Tiny embraced him, feeling as if she was melting in his arms, wrapped in a blanket of love. She could feel their hearts connecting and felt a similar sense of recognition with both Ana and Robbie. Even though she had talked more with Ana on the phone, her meeting with Robbie was as peculiar as meeting Ana or Yu-Ka-Na.

Each meeting point was unique, yet carried a familiar sense of recognition, of Remembrance, of coming home and awakening different aspects in each of them.

"I can't believe this is real!" Tiny said. "It's like I'm in a dream. But this is really happening, right?"

"It sure is!" Ana responded as she teasingly pinched her cheek. "Now, let's get inside and show you around your new home!"

KEY CODE: DIVINE MEETINGS

44. PUTTING THE PIECES TOGETHER

The three of them had gathered in the living room on a chilly Autumn afternoon, sitting on a bunch of pillows near the fireplace, each with a cinnamon hot chocolate between their hands.

"Now, let's put the pieces together," Robbie took the lead, wanting to gather all they had discovered about the Six-Crystal. "At the highest level, there is the Six-Crystal in its pure, original form. The original design. And even before that, you could say that we are and come from one and the same source, what I simply like to call 'Source.' But for now, let's focus on the Six-Crystal."

"Before we separate into individual forms, in the higher realms, there is the collective consciousness of the Six-Crystal. And you can't pinpoint six different aspects in that. It's just one form, one consciousness, our essences united into one whole. But we are all able to tap into this collective consciousness."

"Now, if I get it, the Six-Crystal then splits into an infinite number of different forms to explore and experience itself. Endless variations, yet they all have the same design at their core. It's like everything comes out of the Six-Crystal. Every aspect exists at every level of creation, in every dimension. It's spread out across time and space. It's so hard to grasp this and explain. I'm still trying to wrap my head around this."

Robbie paused, then closed his eyes to ease his mind and connect back in with his heart, open to receiving the information instead of figuring it out.

"And all these different forms share the same desire, the same mission — it's all about knowing and experiencing unity consciousness."

His voice got louder as he couldn't ignore his own excitement for this mission. Ana and Tiny absorbed his words, nodding their heads occasionally, silently agreeing, as they had nothing yet to add.

"We exist on all planes and dimensions. Angels, ascended masters, aliens, dragons, fairies, animals, human beings, and forms we can't even imagine. We have counterparts on every level. We now have this human form, but together, we are Remembering these past and future lifetimes, lifetimes in other galaxies and star systems, in other dimensions. We are all of it."

Robbie started repeating himself, but there couldn't be enough words to let the vastness of this reality fully sink into their minds.

"And if we can collapse time," he continued with a big smile, "then all of this exists at the same time. Have existed and will exist become *exists*."

Ana summarised it, and declared with her hot chocolate:

I exist as a human being.
I exist as an animal.
I exist as an angel.
I exist as a galactic being.
I exist as higher self.
I exist as a collective consciousness.
I exist as a Six-Crystal.

"And all are true at the same time," Tiny chimed in.
"It is trippy, right?!" Ana widened her eyes. They chuckled.
"And here we are, the three of us, three parts of the Six-Crystal.

Each representing a different aspect. Each with our own unique Essence." Robbie marvelled at the miracle of them coming together.

"But with the same design," Ana added with lightning speed as she raised her finger, assuming she knew what he was about to say next.

"But there's more — it's not just the three of us. You girls have opened up the connection to the others. Ana, you have felt the Angelic Presence. She has been guiding you in some way. You have Remembered yourself as an angel, which confirms our angelic counterparts."

"Damn, what do they call male angels, anyone?" Ana suddenly wondered out loud. Tiny raised her eyebrows and shoulders, having no clue.

Robbie, in the zone, continued, "And Tiny, you seem to have a direct connection to our galactic counterparts through your connection with Yu-Ka-Na. This means that we each must have a galactic counterpart and that we each have a galactic form as well. And me, I just have the privilege to be connected to the most beautiful human being I know, with whom I get to taste the exquisite Oneness by melting into her body." His comment surprised Ana, making her blush.

Then he continued, with more seriousness.

"These connections are doorways for us to Remember that we are multidimensional Beings. We are more than just this human form. It's crazy to the mind, but we share too many memories of past, future and parallel lifetimes, even beyond life on Earth or this third dimension. And so, I believe it's safe to say that the Angel represents number 4 of our crystal and Yu-Ka-Na is number 5. We don't know their human form yet, but somehow, they are already plugged into our field through your connections. I can feel their Essence."

Energy rises when truth is spoken, and it was as if a light bulb went off in each of their bodies. Everything in the room became more alive.

"YES!" Ana and Tiny responded simultaneously.

"And then there must be number 6. I like to believe we will soon find out more about who he or she is."

"Let's call him or her SiX, with capital S and X," Ana said, determined, with a big smile. Tiny and Robbie smiled back at her, which Ana took as confirmation.

"So, it seems we need three more humans to complete the Six-Crystal," Robbie continued, "and we just have to trust this magnetic pull that magically brought us together will do the same with the others in divine timing. We gotta stop trying to 'phone home' and rest assured that our destinies are intertwined. Those are the pieces that we have. It seems like the pieces are infinite, so multi-layered and multidimensional. I'm not sure if we'll ever be able to Remember all of who we are, or if it's even needed in this lifetime," he concluded.

"Wow, Robbie, I couldn't have made a better summary, that was … amazing," Tiny said.

"And now, what's next?" Ana asked.

"It's just the three of us. So that's where we start. We continue building a field of harmony and unity amongst ourselves first," Robbie responded.

"And the rest will follow," Tiny added, like it was the final sentence of a chapter.

SiX, the formless One, witnessed this conversation, while simultaneously being in tune with its human version. Indeed, the communication lines between them had not been restored, yet it already knew this was soon to come. A perfect unfolding indeed.

KEY CODE: MULTIDIMENSIONAL BEING

45. THE TRIAD IS BORN

As Ana, Robbie and Tiny gathered and came together in the physical world, the first triad was being born and anchored. Simply being together in the same physical space created an amplified field where their unique Essences blended together, forming one whole: the shape of a triangle.

There is something interesting that happens when two become three.

In a duo, there is only the relationship with self and the relationship with the other. Even though this one-on-one connection can provide the playground for infinite dynamics and lessons to be learned, as soon as a third one enters the field grows exponentially.

Imagine a duo, where the energy flows between two hearts and there is just the two-directional stream between the two. When a third Being enters and a triangle is formed, one can imagine that the energy splits and two streams now go out from one's heart to the other two Beings.

It's not that there is a split in energy or in your amount of love, even though it may feel as if your attention needs to be divided. What happens is that everything doubles. There is only more expansion, exchange, potential, resources and love available. When one opens up to operating as a Trinity, one's senses expand to include all three Beings in one's awareness.

In a triad there are four relationships: three duos, and then the connection as a threesome. To have a fully operational and harmonious triad, all connections need to be in resonance and harmony. Otherwise, you end up with a crooked table leg, and thus a wobbly table.

The most interesting phenomenon is that there is the connection between the two others, that one can only witness yet never fully be a part of. It has its own dynamic and exchange. This offers a new dimension in which learning and transformation can happen, through witnessing instead of through direct personal experience. This means you don't have to go through everything yourself and one can quite literally learn from other's mistakes and challenges. This unlocks exponential growth.

Entering a triad holds an invitation to go beyond comparison, competition and jealousy. One has to face issues of unworthiness, of not belonging and needing to be special. Each one has to recognize that each connection has a different flavour, a different intention, a different dynamic and a different type of exchange that wants to happen. Being able to marvel at the love that is expressed in these different connections will only create a bigger field of all-embracing Love that all add to, as well as receive from.

> *When you know how to be with One,*
> *when you know how to be with Two,*
> *when you know how to be with Three,*
> *then you know how to be with All*
> *and you have all the keys that are needed to build a*
> *strong, resonant collective.*

Operating as a triad is a doorway into embodying the beginning stages of unity consciousness.

And Ana, Robbie and Tiny were surely moving in that

direction. The richness and depth of their interactions opened up a whole other way of togetherness. They could see that telepathy would become a natural step for them, as all three now needed less words to explain things, and Tiny was excellent at foreseeing what Robbie's or Ana's response would be, call it knowing someone well or intuition. Fact was, they had started playing together like a harmonious symphony.

It was quite effortless and easy to relate to each other. There was an endless respect and honouring of each other's uniqueness, with no expectations for the other to change or to be something different than what they were. Simultaneously, they were more straight and direct than ever, not tolerating each other playing small or believing in their own limitations.

They would challenge each other, which could cause internal turmoil, but they deeply respected each other. Knowing love was their baseline, they trusted that their actions were well intended. They gave each other space to grow, to fail and fuck up, and get the chance to fuck up again or learn and do it differently. They knew how to not take everything personally nor seriously, allowing themselves to play in the movie of their lives, while simultaneously recognizing its finite nature.

Without realising it, they were exemplifying how to live harmoniously beyond race, gender, religion and background. They naturally looked for a meeting point, while honouring their differences. They had a common vision and mission, each committed to something bigger than themselves, beyond their own life and personal preferences. They were ALL IN, and that made them stick together like super glue.

Three different expressions, coming together as One in this Trinity.

KEY CODE: TRINITY

46. LIKE AN OPEN BOOK

"How do you think telepathy is going to happen?" Ana asked Tiny as they were sitting at Castle Lake. They had been out for a hike, as Ana had an extra day off work and Tiny loved exploring the area. The lake was like a still mirror that had a calming and soothing effect.

For a moment, Tiny closed her eyes to feel into the question. "We first need a willingness to be transparent. Like there is nothing left to hide."

"Imagine that anyone can read your thoughts, your emotions, your energy. Doesn't it scare you a little?" Ana wondered.

"I'm not sure," Tiny responded.

"I don't want people to know how judgmental I can sometimes be. Aren't we all wearing a mask? Even if you think you are being authentic, think of all the times you want to appear stronger and more put together than the actual mess you feel inside," Ana reflected. "Who is really ready for transparency? Don't we still want to protect our self-image and hide our mistakes, our deepest moments of shame, despair, terror, or hate? But the truth is, we've all had an embarrassing moment, we've all experienced heartbreak, have been terrified or wanted to shoot someone to the moon. We're afraid to own up to our human nature, but we all have our own flaws and fuckups. We're so afraid of what others will think, or that they'll judge or ridicule us, but we each have our own ghosts hiding in a closet. So, what is there to be ashamed about?" Ana pondered as she threw a pebble into the water, causing ripples in the still surface.

"I guess the more we can accept and love every part of ourselves, the easier it gets to see others in their greatness and love them in their mess," Tiny said.

"Good point. Transparency is inviting us to hold each other's experience and perspective as equal and valuable, to take it in as information and receive it as another viewpoint," Ana added.

"So, let's stop hiding," Ana jumped in, all excited. "What is your most shameful moment?"

"Well, you go first!" Tiny said firmly.

"Hmmm, well, let's see. I remember I was about eight years old or so. We had just finished a gym class at school and were getting dressed in the locker room. And suddenly, I couldn't hold it any longer and I peed myself. I was too late to run to the toilet. The piss just dripped down my legs. The girls squealed, some with disgust, some just bluntly laughed at me. Of course, by lunch time the whole school knew about it. 'Ana needs Pampers!' some kids laughed. Oh boy, I felt ashamed and wanted to hide in a corner of the playground. And the next few days, I wore two underpants to prevent it from happening again." She laughed at the memory. "That's mine. Now how about you?"

"I am not sure." Tiny was feeling too embarrassed to even tell her story.

"Oh, come on, Tiny. Don't let me be the only one sharing."

She hesitated, afraid of the assumptions Ana would make about her, and soon Robbie would know, and then …

"Come on, speak up!" Ana's impatience was like a fire starter that didn't give Tiny much space to keep her secret to herself.

"Well, I have never had a boyfriend," she stammered awkwardly.

"Okay, fine," Ana played it cool, "so, you've never had sex with a guy, you mean?"

"Yeah," Tiny shyly looked down.

"And you never even kissed a boy?"

"Nooo! Where I come from, all of this is pretty taboo."

"Well, you're only twenty-one, Tiny. Nothing to be ashamed of, and I can gladly help you out with —"

"No! I don't need your help! And please, don't tell Robbie."

"Well, well, so much for transparency, huh?" Ana teased her. "Alright, I won't tell him. I'll let you dare to share it when you're ready, 'cause one day it will come out. No secrets in our house!"

They packed up their stuff and walked back down the trail, ready to go home.

"Thanks for sharing, Tiny. I could see you felt too ashamed to even tell me. But I still love you, exactly as you are. Nothing has changed now that I know your little secret," Ana poked her.

"Thanks, Ana. Same here. I guess we still have a long way to go before we can be fully transparent," Tiny remarked, slightly self-conscious as she realised she would have to overcome her shyness and unease of sharing about personal matters.

"Well then, we better stay together for a looong time," Ana responded as she grabbed Tiny by the arm and reassured her, "we're in this together!"

KEY CODE: TRANSPARENCY

47. WHEN SCARCITY KICKS IN

Ana held the increased utility bill in her hands.

"Dammit!" It was the proverbial last drop that made her cup run over. She had been scraping her money together to pay the rent, utility bills and Robbie's outstanding healthcare bills. Because he hadn't gone back to work since the accident, Ana felt as if all responsibility for running the household was on her shoulders. Her $12 an hour barista job wasn't going to keep sustaining them. Even though she loved the buzzing atmosphere and meeting new people — since their little town of Mount Shasta attracted tourists and spiritual seekers from all over the world — she couldn't imagine doing this forever, but for now, she couldn't even afford to quit.

She walked up to Robbie, who seemed to be resting, or meditating, or napping.

"I am done with this. We can't have her just stay here for free. And are you thinking of going back to work anytime soon?"

For Robbie, it was crystal clear there was no going back to work. The accident had changed his priorities and he was devoted to the unfolding of their collective design.

"I am not planning on going back. I thought that was obvious. What's upsetting you?" he asked.

"We're all gonna have to pitch in. I can't be the only breadwinner if we want to continue living here. Even the fucking electricity bill has now been raised and …" Robbie tried to interrupt her before she went off on a tangent.

"I don't have the answer right now of how to pay the bills, Ana. The truth is that I don't know. But I do trust," he looked her straight in the eyes, his piercing eyes offering a stability that countered his not-knowing. "There is no point in acting without clarity. It seems I have become more comfortable to sit in the unknown until I am moved to act or decide — from clarity, no matter how long that takes. It's not that I don't want to work, but life ain't about working. You know that!"

"But how do we pay the bills? You think I don't want to sit here and chill like you?" Ana said bitterly.

"Well, I'm not the one stopping you or holding you back from that. But the truth is, even if you wanted to, you wouldn't be able to just chill and relax. Wouldn't you drive yourself crazy worrying about money if you just sat still at home, continuously wondering 'but how are we going to pay the bills?'" It was a rhetorical question, but Ana was annoyed. Easy for him to say, given she was the one carrying all the burden.

"What's highlighted — and let's be clear, you're definitely not the only human on Earth who feels this way — is that you don't trust that you're provided for, that you're taken care of."

"You know that just sounds like some spiritual BS right now, and easy for you to say when I'm paying all the bills and you get to be in chill mode," she responded, rolling her eyes.

"Just say if I am right or not — you doubt that you are provided for." Robbie firmly awaited her answer.

"But I am not provided for, if I don't work my ass off!" Ana was getting more frustrated. "The bills aren't magically going to disappear."

"Exactly, there it is. You believe that *you* need to provide for yourself. And again, you're not the only one. Most of the world is living in this constant state of fear and lack and have cemented their belief that it's up to them to make it all happen. You've taken on a level of personal responsibility that brings you more into survival mode than in divine flow. And I'm not falling for it." The discussion got Robbie heated. He took a deep breath before continuing, "I can't unsee what I've glimpsed, Ana. I can't undo what I know deep in my bones. And I just can't go back to work with the aim of making money, in an attempt to keep you or us safe. I wish I could transfer my Knowing or Trust, and maybe it's not only trust, but also breaking through the illusion of lack. 'Cause when you do, all that is left is abundance."

Sometimes, it felt like he was flying high on a cloud where she couldn't reach him. Ana walked away from the conversation, defeated, because if he wasn't going to make money soon, it was still all up to her.

Tiny had only been around Mount Shasta for a few weeks and was still getting used to being on American soil. Life there seemed to be focused upon working harder, better, faster, stronger, and the rhythm felt like a freight train to her nervous system. Luckily, this small town was bathing in an atmosphere of ease, where spiritual seekers and nature lovers felt at peace. She was applying for a visa to study arts, but even if that didn't work out, they were all convinced they would find a way for Tiny to stay in the US, as they all agreed they were meant to stay together. They had each enjoyed the ease that came with living together, as if Tiny had always been a part of their family. While she was waiting for her visa application to be approved, she had been enjoying time in nature and finding inspiration for her art and poetry. Unknowingly, Ana was about to disrupt that ease.

"These lands, the mountain, the waterfalls, the forests, the springs, this place holds so much richness, more than any dollar could give," Tiny joyfully shared her awe for the area.

"I'm gonna need that dollar to pay our rent and utilities, though," Ana responded abruptly, "which brings me to the fact that I wanted to ask you to pitch in."

"Oh, of course, I don't expect to live here for free. I didn't mean to be a freeloader," Tiny immediately apologised. "I don't mind finding a side-job in town. And I have some savings to pay for this month."

Tiny had been saving up for her travels for over a year and wasn't a big spender. She was happy to volunteer to get her basic needs met, like her time at the organic farm where she had a roof above her head and food in exchange for some work. She didn't have a big money drive, more a basic trust that 'All is well.' She had seen the pieces fall in place when she truly wanted something. It wasn't up to her to make it all happen — her higher self would make sure that all the resources lined up. "Can't miss out on your destiny," was what she told herself.

"That's kind, Tiny, and I am not saying you shouldn't if that's what you want," Robbie interjected, "but Ana, I'm not sure if both of us getting a job would actually solve the problem."

"It sure would pay the bills and help me out," she sniffed.

"Sure. That's just the surface level of your problem. The problem I'm talking about is your frenetic fear, to put it bluntly. I'm not letting you put that on our plate when it's just you who's frustrated. You know, we can't just bring our distress to the table and expect the others to solve it. Don't make your problem into our problem, that's not what the collective way has to be. You can bring it to the table, for sure, as something we, as a whole, can look at and resolve. You don't have to hold it to yourself but take responsibility for what is yours. In this case, what is your fear and distrust."

"Oh, for God's sake! I just want to know how we're going to pay the bills, and everything here is turned into 'do your inner work.' Fuck off lecturing me." Pissed off, she raised her voice.

There was no point in entertaining the conversation further, so they finished their lunch in silence while tension filled the air.

KEY CODE: INFINITE RESOURCE

48. And Much, Much More

Robbie knew Ana's fury by now, and knew she needed to let off some steam and be by herself to sort her head out. He wondered what it would take for them to find a meeting point in this situation. It was clear to him he could no longer solve problems like people normally did. Paying the bills was not the actual problem that wanted to be solved. It had just highlighted Ana's 'lack' mindset, one of the most persistent illusions that held humanity trapped. He wanted to let her see that there was no lack to begin with, for that's where true freedom would arise.

Later that evening, they sat on the back porch where they could see the sun set behind Mount Shasta. Ana had calmed down and was willing to do the inner work, as she realised she could forever be stuck in the rat race in an attempt to acquire more money. She was open to hear what Robbie had to say.

"Look for your own personal and direct experience," Robbie started off. "The mind can't fully grasp this and will continue to try and convince you that other people are starving and dying and find proof that there is lack. For now, just focus on your own life experience, as we each have our own path to walk. So, what is lack? If I simplify it: lack means that something is missing. So check your life experience and ask yourself, was there a time when something was *truly* missing in my life?"

Ana closed her eyes and reflected on her past.

"Now," Robbie continued, "I'm sure your mind can come up with a lot of proof of times where you believed you missed something, whether that was money, attention, support, food, anything really. But it's not about what you believed with your mind. Zoom out and check if there was an actual moment where there was lack, meaning something was missing that should have been there." He paused to let the question sink in. Ana exhaled deeply as she let his words settle.

"Let me give an example. There was a time after my dad died, where we almost had no money to pay all the bills. Mayo sandwiches became our favourite lunch, that's right, just mayonnaise on tasteless white bread. If I go back to that moment, I see myself eating that sandwich, sitting alone at the kitchen table while my mum was at work, just staring out in front of me. Instead of continuing to believe that 'I am missing something,' I go back and see that 'I have everything I need and more.'"

"I go back into that moment and check my reality. First of all, I was breathing," he slowed down his speech while feeling every word, "my heart was beating, we still had a roof above our heads, I was able to go to high school, I was wearing clothes, I even had a smartphone, and a mayo sandwich," he chuckled.

"And clearly, even though we struggled to pay the bills, every time I needed food or water, I received it. The proof is in the pudding — I'm still alive. I've always had everything I needed, and more. Even in the moments I believed I needed more money and was convinced I would end up worse without it, my life experience proved me wrong. It's just the fears of my mind that have always painted pictures full of despair, of losing it all and ending up under a bridge or ending up all alone. But whatever moment I go back to in my direct life experience, I *always* had what I needed, to start with the most essential things like air and my heart beating and ... much, much more than that," he paused.

"So now, Ana, do you remember a moment in your life when you were most convinced that something was lacking. Do you recall one?"

"Yeah, when I first moved here after the accident and had to change jobs. The first month, when I didn't yet work at the coffee bar. I had some savings, but was convinced I was running out of money and didn't know how to pay all the bills."

"Cool. Go back to that moment. You saw your bank account going down and had no clue if, and how, you would get more money. Remember the moments you were afraid of what would happen."

She closed her eyes and recalled how scary it had felt at times.

"Now zoom out and see 'I had everything I needed and more.' See how you were breathing, see how you survived, how you got food and water, you still had this roof above your head, see that you had furniture, clothes, a laptop, and whatever else comes into the picture. See how much you had that you didn't even need in that moment — like pillows, and candles or flowers. The only thing you believed you needed more of at that moment was money, but is that actually true?"

"See yourself sitting at home, let's say, having dinner. Did you, in that moment — and hear me out — in that very moment, did you need more money? If I had given you $1000, the truth is, you didn't need it at that moment. You were simply eating. You had everything you needed, at least in that moment, and even more. And clearly, given you are here now, the time you needed the money to pay the rent, you had access to it, because you are still living here. Are you getting a sense of what I am pointing to?"

She nodded. "Damn, it just really hit me ... that I didn't *need* more money in those moments, but I wanted more money, for sure."

"Sure. Wanting more money is different to believing you are in lack, and thus going into fear and survival mode because you feel like you need to save yourself from your worst-case scenario," Robbie said.

"The key is to really be present in the moment. You will never find lack in this Now moment. I would say that lack is always projected into the future — wondering what will happen, what if one day I'll end up without? Check your direct experience in each Now and your reality will have to confirm that abundance is *always Here, Now*. In every Now. And given that there is only Now, abundance is always," he smiled, big time. "When you really get this, you set yourself free from the illusion of lack and you can throw your fears for the future in the bin as well."

Sometimes she wished she could play his words on repeat and hear them again.

"So now, how do you want to be paying our bills?" he teasingly asked.

"Oh, fuck off, Robbie, don't test me. I'm just starting to get it. I guess the answer is I don't need to know right now, and trust that we'll have what we need to pay when we actually need it."

He looked at her, "Imagine you would no longer be afraid, and you indeed would trust 100% that you are and will always be provided for. How different would that be?"

She shook her head. "What wouldn't be different?!"

"I'm sure many would say this is delusional and you can't just trust your way into abundance. Which is true, and why most still miss the point. The point is that there is *only* abundance! It's when you trust that fully that your outer reality can match and reflect that. Trust means 100% trust. If not 100%, then you're still distrusting. It's as simple as that. And ultimately, it's not even about trusting in it — it's lining up with universal law."

Ana sighed out loud as she relaxed her body and sank deeper into her wicker chair. She had some more distrust to clean up, but at least she was determined to start making her way out of the gripping illusion of lack.

KEY CODE: ABUNDANCE

49. A WALK ON THE BEACH

If you saw them walking down the street, you'd see an atypical bunch. Ana with her curly red hair and lots of flair, Robbie, who seemed the average twenty-something male, yet he exuded a sense of peace and had a sparkle in his eyes that not many had, and then there was Tiny, literally tiny, and a little shy and insecure. They were quite the squad, but they didn't care what others would think of them, as they were well aware that most people were 'asleep' and were living their lives 'on repeat.' No way any of them wanted to go back to the life they used to live.

Tiny had been longing to see the ocean, so they went on a day trip to Moonstone Beach. As they were walking along the coastline, Robbie shared his musings.

"People's energy speaks out so loudly. Walk into any city and it's as if you're walking between bodies on autopilot. You can feel who is stressed and busy. You can feel who is depressed and has no juice for life. You can see who is tense, in fear or worried. You know what I mean?"

"And within that sea of disconnect, you sure get to recognize a bright light, someone who is connected to their joy and passion, walking across the street as if they're walking on roses. Or someone who is in love with life, and you see them enjoying the sunshine on their face, someone who is at peace and relaxed, not running around like a headless chicken but flowing with nature's pace. And I watch and observe and take it all in and see the game each one is playing in their life, most ignorant of the fact that they can be the architect or storywriter of their own life, no matter what has happened to them. And I know whatcha gonna say, Ana." She looked surprised, since for once, Ana wasn't planning on saying anything.

"Yes, I do want these people to 'wake up.' I want nothing more than for every Being to Remember their divine nature and get in touch with their passion and their reason for being here, but I don't need to convince anyone. And I definitely don't need to save anyone. All in Divine Timing. Trusting their path. I want to focus on those people who are waking up and are like 'WTF, now what?', who are wanting to change something about their life and ultimately, the world. I believe we become a stronger force when we do that together. When you bring the power of One through the power of many, we create big ripples."

Robbie ended his monologue. There were times nothing else needed to be said, and no response was needed. Ana and Tiny received his truth and allowed his words to ripple out into their inner worlds.

Tiny was quickly captured again by the sound of the waves and wanted to soak up the fresh air and the vastness of the ocean before going back into the mountains. Even when they were together in silence, it was as if so much was being shared without words.

KEY CODE: DIVINE TIMING

50. CHANNEL SIX

Robbie had the simple desire to connect with number 6 of the Six-Crystal, but without any attachment nor resistance. And as such, instant manifestation of a desire can happen. His request was directly answered.

Robbie found a way to communicate with SiX, although it is equally true to say that SiX found a way to communicate through Robbie. He wasn't connecting to its human aspect yet, but with its higher self, a more formless, genderless, neutral aspect that still held individuation, and even seemed like a spokesperson for their collective consciousness as a Six-Crystal. Words of wisdom would just pour out of Robbie as he connected to SiX. At first, the connection started during his morning ritual, so he started writing everything that came through down in his diary, but soon, he became the channel for SiX's higher self to speak to all of them.

To Ana's dismay, SiX would not give away any details she asked, as higher self honoured free will, and other agreements that had been made pre-birth, that could simply be named as divine orchestration. And sometimes, clarity was meant to be covered by the Veil of Forgetfulness, or call it the Way of Confusion.

When they tuned into SiX, a stillness permeated their field that could right all wrongs and simplify life back to divine neutrality. Yet Ana's curiosity and impatience, at times, could break through the still point and throw in another request that all three of them would tune into.

"I know you can't tell us *where* SiX is, *who* SiX is and *how* we can contact SiX, and yet, we really are eager to meet. Is there anything you can share with us today that will develop our connection?" Ana asked with a mix of respect and impatience.

Robbie closed his eyes, and within less than a minute started channelling SiX. "May I remind you, that as you connect to me, you connect to SiX. As you connect to the Six-Crystal, you connect to SiX. As you connect to your own heart, you connect to SiX. As you are One, and indeed, we are One."

"As you receive me Here, Now, open your heart to receive All of me. Even though not through a physical appearance, you are now able to tap into the Essence and blueprint of SiX. For SiX is an aspect of you, therefore, never can be fully foreign or unknown. Retrieve SiX within yourself first, then together as a whole. Remember SiX within the Six-Crystal and that is all that needs to be done, if anything, on your side."

Robbie continued, "I can share today that SiX has set its own Remembrance into motion. I, as SiX, am not asleep, yet I am yet to Awaken to the Remembrance of my own collective nature. SiX is about to Remember it's a part of the Six-Crystal. It has placed all that is needed for that on its timeline."

"And as such, SiX will awaken and the desire for its collective future will ignite its life force to make brand new life decisions. Rest assured this transition is to come, just as it did for you."

"Relax into this Knowing, for your impatience is only a fight with the illusion of time, while we All are already dancing together in infinity."

"I have given all that is needed in this moment and extend my love to all aspects of Self, of Us. May we Remember the Oneness we already are."

In silence, they sat together, eyes closed, letting everything sink in. Then one by one, they went to bed. All that wanted to be shared had been spoken. And simultaneously, that same night, number SiX had a life-altering moment. Another key got unlocked.

KEY CODE: DIVINE NEUTRALITY

51. Unravelling Oneness

"Look at the three of us. It's like we're fire, earth and ice, or something like that," Tiny giggled. "We are so different, yet being together is so hilariously easy. They say opposites attract, well, I guess it's something like that."

"Yes, we are three extremely different Beings and yet, if we shed our Earth suit, drop our identity, drop the beliefs we have about ourselves, if we move closer and closer to our eternal self, to our infinite nature that exists forever and ever, you'll see that what we are made up of is the same. And then it even seems impossible to believe we are separate or different to begin with, coming from the same Source, ultimately, just energy spinning round and round," Robbie pondered as they hiked up to Panther Meadows.

"But that applies to all of us, to all of mankind, to all living things and creatures — basically, to all that exists. So why are we creating this formation? Why this triad? Why a Six-Crystal? Why create a separate constellation within Oneness?" Ana wondered aloud.

Robbie always had an answer ready. "Isn't that the play within creation? My best answer would be that we are creating this formation because that's what our souls set in motion. That's what we specifically chose or designed to experience here on Earth."

"It is a *choice* to create this formation. And I believe it's good to remain aware that what we are creating and experiencing with the three, and later six of us, is a mini-cosmos of what we intend and envision for humanity, as if we're in a mini-play of what we hope the collective future will be like."

"Yes, that rings true," Tiny responded as shivers ran up her spine.

Ana's mind was still boggled.

"So, if Oneness means we are all One, wouldn't it also mean that, simply put, we are All? And we have been All? Maybe that's why some spiritual teachings say 'you are God,' because if you apply the concept of Oneness, how could God be different than you? How could God be something other than you? There would have to be 'two' for that to be true." She knew by now that trying to understand the mysteries of life from the mind level felt constricted and limited, and very opposite to the vast and unlimited truth of her soul.

"Maybe we can ask SiX to share more about what Unity and Oneness is," Tiny suggested.

Their path followed a creek with crystal clear spring water until they reached the upper meadows, where they found an exceptionally scenic spot with gorgeous views of Mount Shasta and Green Butte peeking out above the treeline. They were now about 7,500 feet above sea level, and the meadows were known as sacred land to the locals. Ana couldn't wait to invite SiX to speak again, as she had wanted to crack the code for months, so she proposed they take a break and meditate there together.

After a few minutes, Ana eagerly asked, "SiX, I would like to welcome you into our space. I'd love to understand more about Oneness, or Unity. Is there anything you can share with us today?"

SiX's consciousness had already merged with Robbie's and he received the full download, which he now, word by word, tried to unpack.

"Oneness is the ultimate reality. It is the truth. Can you imagine for a moment what it's like to *only* know Oneness. There is *nothing* else. Imagine it — Oneness is *All* there is."

"If I say that Oneness is all there is, it still remains a mystery to you. In order to experience Oneness, through the principle of contrast, separation was born. Within this play of duality and polarity, you get to know the light through knowing darkness. You get to know Oneness through separation."

> *And then there were two.*
> *Then there was a here, and a there.*
> *A me, and a you. A now, and a then. A we, and a they.*
> *And so on.*

"To experience both sides of the coin only to, in the end, come to the realisation — which is simultaneously a Remembrance — that both sides are part of the same coin, and thus merge the seeming polarities back into One, extracting the virtue, the gift, and the wisdom that wanted to be seen, learned and experienced in every possible way."

> *One Mission. One Desire. One Intention.*
> *One Thread of Light within Creation*
> *that wants to be experienced in Infinite Ways.*
> *An illusion created, only to realise the truth.*
> *An astounding paradox.*

"These clues can't be grasped by the mind but are received and Remembered through the heart. Every fractal, at any point in time, can find its way back to its original Oneness."

"It is enough to be willing to see it. Yet, the *more* you desire to see, the more you yearn for truth, the more you ache to Remember, the larger the pull into Remembrance. Just like the further you pull a catapult all the way back, the further you'll launch your rock."

To Ana, SiX's messages were like encrypted messages; and indeed, the words were only doorways to deeper layers of meaning shared in between the words.

SiX went on, uninterrupted, "Without contrast, without an opposite to Oneness, its realisation in your reality is only limited. That is why life on Earth offers such a vast and wide array of experience, where souls happily choose to incarnate and experience themselves and their truth through contrast and polarity."

"What you call suffering is the needed catalyst for the soul to Remember itself more fully. As such, separation, disconnect, and loneliness are key life ingredients for the soul who wants to Remember unity."

"You can rejoice in the knowing that this experience is only temporary, and that all you desire will be yours once again. And yet, as soon as you enter unity, life as a separate, individual, disconnected living being will be a distant memory that is hard to recall, so as best as you can, enjoy the experience you are having right now as a human being. It's one moment in time. Once it is done, it will collapse back into the All and never happen again, or will be happening infinitely."

"At this point, the Six-Crystal is desired to be experienced as an unfolding, rather than as an instantaneous manifestation. You are *One* with *All,* and simultaneously you are desiring to experience this as a Six-Crystal. To embody it as the Six-Crystal means to move as One within your earthly life. Remembering that within other dimensions the six are already together. The future you desire already exists, it is already here, lived, done and complete."

"If you realised how unique your current opportunity is, it would spark your zest for life. No matter what appears in your reality, you would receive it as a gift of divine perfection imbued in the design that is propelling your life."

Robbie exhaled deeply. Higher frequencies had been flooding his body, making him a little lightheaded. He wasn't sure if he had been able to clearly transmit and translate the download he had received, yet he trusted the words that flowed through his mouth as he connected to SiX.

And Ana, she was still stunned. "Thank you, SiX, for being here with us and for all you shared. I'm not sure if I now understand more about Oneness. But I do know that it's my life's work to find out and 'innerstand,' so let's enjoy the ride!"

Life went on and there was magic in simply being together. They didn't always notice themselves how compatible they were, nor that they brought out the best, and sometimes worst, in each other.

Robbie became more aware that the Six-Crystal was full of craziness, or in other words 'geniusness', and that it was up to him to support each Being to fully recognize their own greatness and turn their hidden and untapped potential into thriving abilities that would serve the whole and all of humanity.

Tiny felt really seen by Robbie. It was as if he could look right through her. He had supported her to further explore her singing and toning, and she had started to not just write poetry, but also music. "Music that will soothe the soul!" she called it. Talking to Robbie had already helped her gain more confidence, even before they had come together. It was clear she had more abilities to uncover, but she was happily taking it step by step.

While Robbie was the bridge on a more cosmic, multidimensional level, able to most easily tune into SiX and channel information, Ana was the bridge on a more earthly, practical level. She knew how to take the wisdom that was given and make it into more practical concrete steps, and even practices they could do. She inspired them to change their daily routines and align their daily life to their highest good, both individually and collectively.

Ana was also, no surprise, the most expressive one. If ever they had the desire to communicate or share their story with the world, undoubtedly it would be Ana taking the lead. She loved talking, and she had more recently been in touch with the desire to keep track of, and one day share, this magical unfolding. She wanted people to see what happened in their lives, as things were about to get even more magical, she was absolutely convinced of that.

It couldn't just stay a fantasy. She could write a book about it, but she was sure that most people would believe it was just fiction and she chuckled at the idea of that. She wanted people to *see* their lives. She wanted people to *see* what was up next, given that what had happened so far had already been quite extraordinary. Pretty soon, she would become a vlogger to capture their collective journey.

KEY CODE: PRINCIPLE OF CONTRAST

52. THE REDWOODS

"I want to go on a journey together," Tiny proposed.

"You mean like a trip, Tiny?" Ana asked. They had just watched a documentary about psychedelic mushrooms, so Ana thought of a magic mushroom trip.

"Yes! We can take a trip. There is this place that's calling me, and we have to go there all together," Tiny replied innocently.

"What is it? Wonderland?" Ana couldn't help but be silly.

Tiny frowned.

"No, Ban-Ana," Tiny teased her back, "I believe we have to go on a trip and go to the Redwoods. It's like a treasure hunt. I don't know why, and I don't know anything about it. All I know is that this location is the next clue and we've got to follow it!"

"Well, detective," Ana responded mischievously, "how do you know we have to go to the Redwoods if you don't know anything about it?"

"My bottle of soap just confirmed it," Tiny said firmly. She knew this would be totally nonsensical, but she had come to trust her own sensing and how her higher guidance showed her next steps.

"Your bottle of soap, ha," Ana repeated with a big grin.

"Well, I have been seeing the name Redwoods pop up a few times. First on an ad in the grocery story, then scrolling on Instagram, and now, on the new bottle of soap I picked up. It's called Redwood 'with an exhilarating scent of coastal woodlands.' If it appears three times, that's just pure confirmation to me." Tiny was very decisive.

"And you want all three of us to go?" Ana wondered.

"Of course! I'm not doing this on my own, you know. We're in this together This is *our* adventure. Our mission. Our mystery," Tiny declared.

Ana sometimes felt like she was part of a superhero squad, although it would be more correct to say she was part of a group of misfits and crazy ones, as they didn't have dope superhero skills, yet they had a touch of magic, nonetheless.

"You're right. There's no way I would let you go off on your own, missy. Imagine you meet Yu-Ka-Na in the flesh. I wouldn't wanna miss that! Please let me be there when you do!" She grabbed Tiny by the arm as if it was up to her to decide.

Tiny couldn't imagine what it would be like to meet him, or if it was even possible, or if she would recognize him, or vice versa. Thinking about it made her head spin, so she made a big sigh and repeated, "All I know is we need to go to the Redwoods."

∗

"I have been here," Tiny spoke quietly as she walked the land lightly with a sense of déjà vu but amplified ten times. It was as if she was walking into the movie studio of a scene she had already played in, yet this time aware of that fact. She looked as if she was afraid to crush it by walking in it.

"What is she talking about?" Ana looked to Robbie, who just shrugged his shoulders.

Tiny looked up to the redwood trees, with their red-brownish trunks reaching over 350 feet high up in the sky. She felt a deep reverence as she stood next to these giant pillars of wood. It was easy to feel tiny and imagine her own life passing by in just a second, compared to the trees that had been standing there for over two thousand years.

"I recognize this place. I have been here before. *We've been here before.*"

"Mmm, no, never been here before, missy!" Ana responded with certainty.

"I get it, it's my first time here in this forest too. It's my first time in the US. But it's not, Ana!" she exclaimed. "We have been here before!" her voice got louder in the hope Ana would also Remember, or at least understand what she was implying.

Ana was about to repeat herself, when Robbie suggested, "Let's connect to the land, ladies. Let's dive in together and see what is here."

They each found a spot and sat with their back against one of the giant redwood trees. They couldn't have done it if they had tried, but they naturally formed a pretty symmetric triangle with angles of about 60°.

They each planted their feet firmly on the ground as they wanted to connect more deeply to the Earth, grounding themselves through their root and opening a channel of exchange and communication with the land and the trees, simply through intention. Automatically, they also synced up their energy with each other, forming one whole, one web, one trinity.

As they tuned in, they each gathered pieces that, when brought together, would form a more cohesive whole and could give more insight about what soon wanted to be understood and experienced there.

One after the other, they shared what they felt, while keeping their eyes closed, as if they were throwing pieces of wood on a campfire.

Robbie, "We have been here before, not in the past, but in our future. It was a glimpse of the future, Tiny!"

Ana, "We are here to plant the seeds."

Tiny, "The tree network is holding and storing information that we are tapping into. These trees have built a powerful underground network. I can sense how their roots are connected. As we tap in and unify, we also sync up, energetically, with this information."

Ana, "It's like we are bringing something down, from the cosmos, and anchoring it through these trees and through their roots into the earth."

Tiny, "We are anchoring the collective template into the earth. These ancient trees are connected and spread across the globe. This could also be done through the water or through the air, but for some reason, it wanted to be done through the earth element. I sense it's because these redwoods are some of the oldest trees here in the US."

As they shared all the pieces, they understood what was going on, yet their minds didn't really get it.

"So, why are we coming back here? And when?"

"What about the seeds being planted? And our collective template?"

More questions were left unspoken and unanswered.

Robbie invited them to not try and grasp it with their minds. "What's your heart telling you?"

"We did exactly what we needed to do," Ana replied. "There has been a lot of exchange, like we're uploading and downloading information simply by being here. More and more, at least when I feel into my heart, I understand there is so little I understand with my mind, yet in my heart it is obvious and known, fully understood, even if I can't explain it or put it in words. And that's okay. So much is happening here beyond what we can see."

"Yes, I can feel that." Tiny was shaking slightly and shivering. The time jump she had just experienced had moved her deeply, not just because she was receiving more and more premonitions and foresight, but because she had felt what it was like to be together in the future. And there was a whole other level of Oneness, of deep Fulfilment, of Harmony, of Peace, of Gratitude, and just pure Love that seemed to be a natural part of her existence, that tasted so sweet it touched her heart and left her in a slight overwhelm of feeling 'so much goodness.'

They knew they would be back there one day; they just didn't know when yet. They had all been embracing the unknown more and more, walking through life like the fool of the tarot deck, who walks his path with pure innocence and full faith, not worried about what's to come but staying fully present in the moment, trusting he will be carried and supported every step of the way. Embodying Trust was a key to come into Oneness as their lived reality.

KEY CODE: FUTURE GLIMPSES

53. PURE INTENT

The Trinity had gathered again in the living room. As the sun was setting, its golden rays beamed through the window, creating a cosy atmosphere. Ana would soon light some candles to make sure they could continue seeing each other. Yet, they all enjoyed sitting in the twilight.

Somehow, they had found a way to know when the next meeting with SiX would occur. They didn't have to discuss this, as they all would feel a similar pull to come together and tune in to their collective field.

Robbie opened up his channel, and naturally SiX's higher self plugged into his consciousness for him to be the spokesperson for what wanted to be shared next.

SiX seemed like a guide and wisdom keeper and shared some valuable life lessons that held unique invitations for each of them. Today, it was all about stepping into their divine power.

Robbie, as SiX, shared, "The Power of Creation is seeded in each individual, yet when combined as a collective force, it quite literally is a force that could move mountains. When the power of One becomes the power of We, all lingering individual distortions can come to the surface and are more rapidly dissolved by a pure, direct and potent stream of unconditional love. For this power to be activated in your collective, each aspect, and thus each individual, needs to investigate its relationship to power. It's common to fear one's own power and the responsibility that comes with it."

"Because just as this force has the ability to create worlds, so too can it destroy worlds. Many of you carry imprints of past life imbalances and you are invited to allow all guilt, shame, trauma and pain that still resides within your body-mind-spirit vehicle to be felt and resolved."

SiX continued without a break, "You all hold the memory of Atlantis in your DNA. This is where power was first used to thrive, then later misused, causing the collapse of an entire reality."

"When one is blinded by power and desire turns into greed, power turns into overpowering and disturbs the natural balance of Creation."

"It is important to see how all of this played out in divine orchestration, and to realise that one has learned from the past and your current mission is not to repeat what has been. Reclaiming and embodying your power does not entail overpowering and abusing other-selves and other lifeforms."

It felt as if SiX was now directly talking to them. "One has to look deep within. Check yourselves. Ask yourself if you are here to do harm, cause hurt, overpower or destroy."

"Clear the residue of past memories and free yourself. Then see your Pure Heart and your Pure Intent, your service and dedication to a Greater Good."

"Once you Know your purity, much of your self-doubt can fade away and you can rest assured knowing that you are part of this collective mission, here to bring forth a new iteration and a new play where your divine power can be embodied again, and the balance of life can be restored. This is neither done through overpowering *nor* by denying your true power."

As usual, Tiny and Ana were just receiving SiX's waterfall of words, allowing the message and wisdom to enter their hearts. As always, it felt like too much to take in for their minds, while simultaneously, they each got their next step, their next clue of what inner work needed to be done.

But SiX was not done yet. "It seems there is either a denial or a fear of power rising within you, or both. This journey cannot be understood by the mind, as it sweeps the ground under your feet when it comes to what identity and belief systems the mind has built."

"We can assure that the needed shifts will take place slowly, meaning, you only open up to what you can handle in that moment. Still, your minds will be blown and your body's nervous system needs to be well taken care of. It is important that you find a baseline of safety within and dissolve most Earth-related fears, and thus clean up your relationship to being as powerful as you truly are, before any ability will open up."

"Again, look deep within you, to see that this Six-Crystal is encoded with pure intent. Anything less shall not pass through. It is impossible for any one of you, and together as a whole, to intentionally harm, hurt or destroy. You are Here to set forth a harmonious, coherent, resonant co-existence with All living Beings so All can Thrive. 'ALL can Thrive.' — that is the Truth, and that is the North Star."

"There is no leaving anyone behind. All souls have chosen their part in this play, and if they continue to exist and stay alive on Earth, then trust their awakening and activation sequence will turn on in their divine timing."

"Even if you can't fully understand what divine orchestration means, see how it has played out in your own life's journey, then, see how it played out for those around you, and last but not least, trust and transfer this Knowing onto all other living beings. This will save you lots of headaches, worries and judgments."

Ana was curious and wanted to understand. "SiX, you mentioned that we have to clean up our fears before our abilities open up. What does this mean?"

Robbie received the question and stayed in a receptive mode, keeping his mind empty while awaiting the answer that SiX wanted to share. "It is impossible for you to see all that this entails, as it is beyond your wildest dreams and taints your logical mind of what you have believed to be possible or impossible. Even though you all are already open-minded, still your minds have been confined by your current 3D matrix and the limits of your current space/time perceptions. Yes, the Six-Crystal activation includes the restoring and reactivating of many forgotten abilities that can be found in historic texts, yet often have been depicted as magical, as unreal or unreachable."

"These abilities are no longer kept secret in the mountain caves of the gurus, nor only available to certain mystic lineages and mystery schools. It is your birthright to Remember and Reclaim these as your collective wisdom. Yes, open yourself to see, experience and witness these abilities coming online. The following are primed within your collective to come first: telepathy, time bending, levitating and bilocation."

From SiX's perspective, these were just another set of skills, while to the human mind these would be seen as supernatural.

SiX continued, "Can you see that all your visions hold truth? Why do you, Tiny, think you have an undeniable fear of heights? You've dreamed of flying since you've been a child, but your higher mind had to install a safety mechanism that would keep you from jumping out of a window as long as that skill is not yet online. So your higher self adjusted your dream to fly, in other words, your Remembrance of that ability, and infused it with fear of heights, given you've been bound by gravity up till now."

The doorbell rang and interrupted their gathering. Clearly, enough had come through for them to sit with.

Ana checked the door, "I guess just children playing knock,

knock, ginger. No one there. So, guys, what do you think? Time for levitating?"

"I feel that we have to look deeper into this power theme," Tiny looked pale. "When I went to Egypt, I had these flashes, like memories, of being a pharaoh, then later seeing Cleopatra, and I just, I see how power has been so often misused in history. I'm still afraid to say I am powerful or to even want to claim it. It feels like power itself is like a powerful substance. And yet, through SiX's sharing, I can see what power actually is. It's just the pure force of Creation — it is *life*! Isn't it that divine power that makes my heart tick and the flowers grow? I just wouldn't have called that power."

"To see myself in power," Tiny continued, "is to see how I am a creator. And yet, I have been taught I can't play nor compete with God. To even think I'm omnipotent would mean blasphemy or having a God complex. Humbleness is a greater virtue. I hear what SiX is saying, but I don't know yet how to fully resolve this inner conflict."

Ana shared next. "Let's also not forget to check our 'purity'. Just that word is enough to make me remember how the church has wanted us to believe we are sinners. When I think of my purity, what comes up are all the mistakes I've made. It's like it brings up shame and guilt and self-blame, as if somehow, I am already convinced that I am not pure."

"Yes, it seems that we all have our own inner work to do, ha," Robbie said. "I do resonate better with the words 'pure intent,' rather than purity. Pure intent reminds me of the intention that is fuelling all I am and do. And it's true, Ana, we've all made mistakes. I think we fully need to take responsibility for all the harm and hurt we have caused. Be honest if you betrayed your ex. Be honest if you lied to your friend. Be honest if you were selfish. Own your shit and it will stink less." They all burst out in laughter.

"Seriously," he said, "we're letting go of that shit by acknowledging it for what it was, and seeing why we did what we did, realising that our younger self did not have the capacity, ability or insight to act differently. But as we shed these layers, and as SiX mentioned, when we turn our gaze within, we get to see that at our core, there is *only* Pure Intent." To Ana, Robbie was as wise as SiX.

He continued, "I know deep within that there is not one hair on my head that intentionally wants to hurt another human, or animal, or planet, or alien for God's sake. The more we realise Oneness, the more we get that causing hurt is only creating harm to yourself. Not just as an idea, but as a felt experience. Why on earth would I want to harm or hurt myself? How can I turn on myself? It only happens within the Veil of Forgetfulness. I don't think that a woke creature can continue to rape itself like humanity has raped our Earth."

Ana had to interrupt, "Phew, guys, thank you for sharing, but that's enough for me in one day. I can't take any more of this. Peace out. I'm heading to bed." She swiftly got up, then stopped as she turned around and said more softly, "Also, thank you for being here with me, you know, this is really special."

KEY CODE: PURE INTENT

54. WAKE-UP CALL

One day, SiX will pick up a Book that will instantaneously alter its life course. SiX will discover through the Book who it is and why it's here.

Even though SiX's mind and mental body will not yet be able to grasp the potency and portal of the Book, and therefore might see it as a fictional or impossible story, undeniably, the course will be set in motion and its transmission will enter SiX's Light Body. This Book is encoded with all the keys and information needed to activate a specific sequence in SiX's DNA to unlock its Remembrance. Nothing can be done to stop it.

The Book is already placed in SiX's hands and divine orchestration is at play.

If SiX is able to pierce through the veil while reading, it will be accompanied by activation on all levels and in all bodies: energy waves, tingles, chills, heat, cold, tears, recognition and heart opening are all physical symptoms that may occur. This is not even necessary. The Book itself is the key.

Something will unlock that doesn't make sense to the mental body, but the veil will be pulled from SiX's eyes.

There is no seeking SiX.

SiX will find you.

It is inevitable. Like the magnetising force of two poles that are drawn to each other, so will SiX be magnetised to this field to complete it, also in physical form. And when it does, a whole new world will open up. When completion and wholeness is reached as a Six-Crystal in physical form, you will be able to tap into a cosmic power that has long been forgotten, a power that goes back to times where what you call Gods or Star Beings were still able to freely roam around on Earth.

✱

Ana stared at the ceiling. It was 2:00 a.m., but she couldn't sleep. The last transmission of SiX was playing on repeat in her head. She thought it was a miracle how she had found Tiny, but this was a whole other level of magic. Divine orchestration reached a whole other level of possibilities she had never seen before. She started to see more and more how this was not done by some outer force or power, but a well-designed orchestration that her own higher self and her collective as a hive mind had set in motion.

She was curious — had the human version of SiX already read the Book? Or maybe SiX was even reading it right now? Or maybe the Book would just disappear on a bookshelf. She wondered who had written the Book and what it was about. She had so many questions, but one thing was for sure — there was nothing she could do to *find* SiX. This was out of her hands.

Sometimes, it was better to leave things up to that higher power that knows how to create life, and so, the only thing left for her right now was to try and go back to sleep.

KEY CODE: DIVINE ORCHESTRATION

55. FALLING APART

As much as they moved into harmony and love together, at times, the pendulum swung to the other side and brought up deep pain, wounds and limiting beliefs that were still held in their nervous systems. That's when their pain bodies matched, and they became the perfect mirror and trigger for each other to fall back into their core beliefs of unworthiness.

This was part of the unfolding. Everything that didn't match the vibration of unity could not continue to exist. They had set the intention to unify, and now everything that was not aligned was coming to the surface to be seen, cleared and integrated, resolved and reconciled, so they truly could move as One. When shit hit the fan, they themselves couldn't always see the divine plan of this unfolding and got lost in their own stories and drama. And so it happened that they were brought to their knees, gearing up to a breaking point, where they appeared unable to hold their unity as their truth and direction.

Ana had the opportunity to return to the corporate world, with an invitation to work as an interior designer for a new and innovative start-up. She had been dreaming of such an opportunity for years before the accident, and now it was right in front of her. She would earn at least triple her earnings as a barista but would have to move to Los Angeles to make it work. The distress of her low wage had been too much to handle at times in recent months, so this felt like a gift sent from heaven. However, Ana's opportunity not only shook the outer foundation of their lives together, but also caused turmoil in their inner worlds.

Robbie hadn't been back to work since the accident, but he felt deeply at home near Mount Shasta and had no intention of moving back to a city, especially not a big city like Los Angeles. And then there was Tiny. She was not in charge of this choice point, and yet whatever was decided would influence her life directly. She had no intention of going back to Taiwan, but when Ana discussed the job offer, she never mentioned or accounted for Tiny in her plans.

The question had been in the air, unspoken for a while now, and the time was coming that Ana had to make a choice.

"Guys, I have to make a decision. This is like a turning point in my life. If I don't do it, it feels like I will regret it forever. But if I do, I'm gonna have to leave this town, and Robbie, we're gonna have to start a long-distance relationship if you don't want to leave Shasta. I don't want to regret this for the rest of my life. What am I gonna be doing instead — continue being the best barista in this town? That's not my ultimate goal. I want to get more out of my life. I feel like I want to be rebuilding my career and get a stable financial foundation, and then buy a home and …"

Ana went off on a tangent. She was repeating everything she had learned about what it means to be a 'successful,' independent woman. Blinded by the image, she simply didn't take into account what the others, or the whole, wanted.

Tiny felt extremely sad. She felt alone, unmet. Witnessing Ana, she couldn't understand what was happening. It was as if Ana had shifted into a different reality. How was it possible that the Six-Crystal suddenly seemed unimportant and didn't matter? Suddenly, all Ana cared about was her career, status, and her own success. Tiny didn't know this version of Ana and felt deeply disappointed. Tiny had felt she'd found her soul tribe, and that they had a shared mission that was their number one priority, but now Ana just wanted to take off on her own.

Tiny's hurt made her withdraw. She played her poker face to protect her heart and swallowed her truth and sadness. A ticking time bomb filled with suppressed emotion.

Robbie had anchored in such a deep state of trust that he was just letting it all happen. He didn't understand it either, yet he trusted more in divine orchestration than in what was playing out in front of his eyes. He was able to relax into a deeper stream of faith underneath the surface. He had questioned her, talked to her, challenged her, but still she kept coming back to wanting this seemingly dream job.

Robbie did feel heartache. He too felt that Ana was opting for a separation of sorts, instead of a deeper commitment to their trinity. How would they continue to move as One while apart?

Even though their Unity and Oneness, on a multidimensional level, didn't change, it felt clear to him they were destined to embody, live and move as One in a more practical, earthly way. He had no clue how that would be possible if she was nine hours away. Yet instead of getting caught up in the details, Robbie wondered what was actually happening. What was playing out here? What wanted to be seen and revealed? He believed they were still moving towards more unity; he just couldn't see yet how this too was perfect.

And Ana was definitely being seduced by her dreams of the past. To get this job offer, something she had been wanting for so long, she felt she couldn't refuse it. It felt like if she said no, life would never again give her what she wanted, like she somehow had to be grateful, accept it and go for it, in order to get what she wanted in life. And yes, she was willing to give up everything for that.

Her choice was also influenced by a slight and sneaky doubt that had entered her mind. It had been a while since Tiny joined them, and even though they had been communicating with SiX, the others were still in the invisible realms. Ana had begun doubting the possibility of the others joining them in real life.

This job was real, while the Six-Crystal was still a mysterious and intangible thing — what if they had just made it up? There was no certainty or guarantee in it. What would it bring her? What would it give her in life? It sure wouldn't be paying her bills. Twisted and turned, she felt she couldn't let this opportunity slip away, and somehow, she still hoped to make her dad proud, as he would approve of this job over her barista job at the local coffee bar.

Robbie initiated the discussion.

"Ladies, let's get it out in the open. I can feel there is something brewing. From being close and loving like sisters, you now barely talk to each other. Tiny, you shy away, and Ana, you just — all you do is think and talk about your job offer. Like, what's going on? Let's speak about it."

He looked at Ana and Tiny. Tiny's downcast eyes made it clear her introverted nature would prevent her from opening up first.

Ana sniffed, already offended, as if she had been called to court while she didn't feel like she was doing anything wrong.

"I just don't feel supported. This is not even about Tiny. It's just, this is such a big opportunity for me, and it feels like no one is getting it. I have to figure this out alone, and I don't feel like either of you are supporting my choice. I feel like you both just want me to stay here, and what — keep on doing what we're doing, which is what exactly? Hoping more Beings miraculously show up at our doorstep?"

Robbie noticed the tears welling up in Tiny's eyes. "Tiny, how are you feeling?"

"I am just really sad. Since Ana, since you got that job offer, it's like there is a distance between us. It's like you're in a different reality. I can't talk to you. You are just on your job offer cloud. It's as if the Six-Crystal … as if none of it matters … as if I don't matter. I just hide in my own cave. What can I say? What can I do? How would it matter? It doesn't," she wept. "I don't want to stop your dreams. If you feel like that job is what you want, then go for it. I just don't understand — I thought we all wanted the same and felt the same. I thought we wanted to explore what living in unity means, that we wanted to move together and start creating together, whatever that would be. And you're just veering off in a whole different direction. It just breaks my heart. It's like popping a balloon and the dream just ended."

Tiny felt some relief just being able to pour her heart out and share what she had been holding for too long.

Ana didn't like seeing Tiny in tears. She needed some space to think.

"I don't know what to say right now. I need some time to think. I can't do this." She fled out the door, running away from her own tears and the whole conversation. Tiny looked at Robbie, wondering if she had made a mistake sharing her heart.

As if he could read her question, he just said, "It's okay. It's gonna be okay, Tiny. Let's just give her some space. She'll come back when she has sorted it out for herself."

KEY CODE: BREAKING POINT

56. WATERFALLS

Ana drove for four hours, back to her favourite ocean spot, where she had Remembered the Six-Crystal. There, she felt free enough to let her tears flow and give them back to the water. It felt as if she was faced with the biggest choice point of her life.

She could choose the job, a long-time dream, and aim for success and the financial security she would need to build her life, buy a home, and maybe even make her dad a little proud.

OR …

Choose the unknown, the Six-Crystal, their trinity and go for unity. She had no clue what was next, how to do it or what would happen. Choose the full-on mystery, with no security or certainty, and no guarantees.

This option scared the shit out of her!

Ana was scared of losing herself in this unity. She wanted to have and keep some control of her life, but she could feel that was not what her soul was inviting her into. It felt like she had to give up and surrender.

Surrender. A word she had been reading in so many of her spiritual books. Now it felt like she was brought to her knees to give up all she had ever deemed important and instead, follow her inner compass that sometimes spoke so subtly, yet simply and directly.

There was no guarantee and no road to success. Ana felt the fear creep in. She was afraid to be a failure, to fail at life — but who had made up the rules of what winning and failing at life looked like?

The ideas of what success in life means didn't take into account soul fulfilment and one's higher purpose, and certainly not a greater design like the Six-Crystal. She had been blinded by the 'bling bling' potential of success, clinging onto some sense of security and a false sense of safety, wanting to play in the game of life according to what she had been told to be and do.

Instead, this choice point asked her to take the biggest trust fall.

Saying *NO* to this job offer, felt like saying *YES* to her soul.

Saying *YES* to the Six-Crystal and committing, over and over again, to their trinity and unity.

It felt like saying yes to the unknown, yes to trusting life, to her higher self and to divine orchestration, which her mind couldn't fully grasp. It felt like saying yes to doing life in a completely different way, to carve out a new pathway, a new way of being and operating, which she would only discover with every step she took.

Something inside pulled her to choose this path. Life with no compromise, with no regret, with her design and purpose in the lead, no matter what it takes, no matter where it leads, being fully open to the mystery.

Tears streamed down her face like waterfalls. She understood she had to give up Her-Self — the self she had built and had become, the image of a strong, independent, successful woman. But it was nothing but an image, a character, a role an actress could take on. If she was honest, it was a costume she had been told to wear, but it didn't suit her that well.

She was way more free, eccentric, and strong-minded than most, so there was something epic about pioneering a new way. It wasn't about succeeding or getting somewhere, but simply *living* it. Choosing it. Going for it. The journey is more important than the destination — and what a ride she was on!

There at the ocean, her heart said yes. Her soul had already said yes. And after considering what she truly wanted in life, her mind said yes too. Ana gave her tears back to the ocean, releasing with them her old dreams and expectations.

Ana knew she had to 'get over herself' more, as she had been quite self-centred in her life, and she knew the day was coming that she had to dissolve this and return to a selfless way of being, where the whole was the highest good, not just her own big or little dramas, or her own needs and desires.

And yet, she was starting to understand and believe that the Highest Good of All embraced her true desires. Maybe not what her mind or ego wanted, but what her soul wanted and desired. The highest good included what was best both on an individual and collective level.

"I will not die before we have lived this collective potential!" she declared with her feet in the surf of the ocean. Her voice was loud and clear, solid and grounded, her heart open and loving. She felt hopeful and excited for the future. She knew there would be three more human beings who would show up and reveal themselves as the others of their template. Then the fun could really begin! The Six-Crystal would become a living template, and that was only if you believed time to be a linear thing. Without that, it was already lived, it was already done.

She felt a little foolish as she returned home, but Robbie and Tiny embraced her with a cloak of love. They knew how tough this choice point had been for Ana, and all that mattered was to feel her truth.

Ana felt it was the bravest decision she had ever made when she turned away her dream job. She knew her family would believe she just went crazy, but her soul, her higher self, her guides and angels in the upper realms were all celebrating and cheering her on. She noticed the white butterfly that passed by as she hung up the phone after saying no to the job offer.

Ana smiled, for she knew, "All is well."

KEY CODE: THE HIGHEST GOOD OF ALL

57. Heaven on Earth

"I'm receiving more future glimpses."

Tiny couldn't wait any longer to share this with Ana and Robbie.

"It's foggy and dreamy, and just these short bursts of images, like a glimpse. It's as if you're getting just a snapshot of a movie scene, but the picture contains everything you need to know. It feels as if all the information is in there, and yet, it feels like the greatest mystery, because it disappeared as soon as it came into my vision. I try to repeat it and replay it in my mind, but there is no doubt that I'm adding assumptions and ideas onto what I actually saw. I try to make sense of it from my current perspective and understanding of the world."

"What did you see?" Robbie asked.

Tiny sighed out loud, followed by two seconds of silence.

"It's like I am seeing Heaven on Earth. I have no better way of summarising it."

A big smile appeared on Robbie's face. "Heaven on Earth. What are you seeing that makes you say that?"

Another sigh, this time less loud.

"I see us living in nature. We are not in a city. And there is just something about the Earth and the land. It's so alive and vibrant. It feels as if it's bursting with liveliness. We really are living together *with* nature, like in a partnership. The land we live on informs us about what's possible, what we can build there, how we can live there, its resources, the weather, the plants — everything informs us."

"And we do live in these beautiful houses. It's not that we live like cavemen. I saw glimpses of the most magnificent and beautiful organic structures. I see more wave-like and rounded forms built with natural materials, but everything is so pretty. It's just amazing how pristine it is, and at the same time, it's with so much respect for the land."

"Every piece in my house is 'on point.' It's either practical or needed, or it just lights me up, but there is no waste or overconsumption or anything like that. And yet, nothing is missing. It feels more abundant than anything I've ever seen, and yet most people would have to empty out their houses and take only 20% of what they have." She laughed, "It's ridiculous, but true."

"Mmm, I *love* what you are seeing, Tiny," Ana commented, feeling the sweetness of Tiny's vision.

"And, it's Heaven on Earth because of how we live together. Not just our Six-Crystal, but this wider community we are a part of, or this village, I don't know what it is. I see it for the whole world, but I don't know if that's realistic. It seems there are so many things that no longer exist in these future glimpses I'm getting."

Tears welled up in her eyes, evoked by a combination of her longing for a better future and sadness for humanity's suffering.

"There is no jealousy or competition. I can't imagine people fighting or having arguments or yelling at each other. There's no betrayal, or lying, or anything like that. They live in honour, with respect for self, for everyone around them, for the Earth and the animals. They live in harmony, in peace, in love, with joy, gratitude, and appreciation. It's like everyone is thriving. Everyone is living out their … I guess their potential. It's like everyone is shining and radiant, and has this spark of life that I see in your eyes too, Robbie, but then a hundred times stronger. It just radiates from their whole body. It's like we are Divinity walking around."

Robbie and Ana received her words like a sweet melody entering their hearts.

"There's no hierarchy. I don't see a guru or a king, or a leader, or someone at the top who is worshipped or followed. It feels like this is everyone's kingdom and queendom — simultaneously. Everyone is creating — thriving — simply BEing. It sounds so naive, but it is *so* beautiful! I so badly want this to be true. I *want* this to happen. And I have no clue how or if it's possible. Seems impossible if I think about how people are living right now." The sadness won and she burst into tears and ran into Robbie's arms for a hug. But Remembering Heaven on Earth was all that was truly needed in that moment.

KEY CODE: HEAVEN ON EARTH

58. UPGRADING THE SIX-CRYSTAL ACTIVATION

"I got another download!" Tiny was excited as she had found new pieces to share. "When I was in that meditation simultaneously with Ana, the first time we met in the invisible realms, yet where we kinda showed up in each other's reality, remember?" Ana nodded with certainty. As if she could ever forget!

"I felt Ana as this *Red,* more fiery presence. And Robbie, when I sense you, it's like you are *Blue.* And then, I don't know, it might be because of my connection with Egypt, but I see myself as *Yellow.*"

"Now you see, those are the three primary colours. So, then I thought, eventually we will be with six, and that would mean we need three more colours. Can you guess it — the secondary colours, of course! That felt like a truth bomb, so I felt into it, and randomly I would say that Yu-Ka-Na is *Green,* the Angelic Presence is *Purple,* and our mysterious SiX then would be *Orange.*"

Robbie couldn't help but smile as he continued to be amazed by Tiny's multidimensional way of seeing.

"Now, the thing with these colours is that we can be *all* colours. We *are* all colours. Is this making sense or am I just rambling?" she interrupted her own flow.

"Yes, yes! Go ahead," Ana encouraged her. Robbie nodded, with his typical sturdiness.

"So, three primary colours, three secondary colours, that is six. Oh yeah, we hold all colours, but then, it may just be that there is one colour that naturally fits us a little more. So, what if we now added these colours into our Activation Ritual of the Six-Crystal?"

"Colour is light, and Light is the beginning of Creation," Robbie added.

Tiny continued, "So we are connecting to each aspect through its original form of the Six-Crystal, as pure white Light that then splits into six aspects."

Six different colours,
Six different Essences,
Six different Beings.

"And even though we don't know yet who the three other human beings are, we know their colour, which means we know their Essence as Light." Tiny ended her presentation with a big smile, proud of this revelation.

Ana almost expected her to make a bow.

"That's a great idea, Tiny! You keep on surprising me, for sure. What do you think, Robbie?"

"I say this girl is a genius, although if someone else would hear us they would think we're trying to make a rainbow. Well, we are, aren't we? Together we are all colours of the rainbow. Together we are One — white Light."

That evening they sat down in a triangle, repeating the Activation Ritual Ana and Robbie had created months ago. Tiny had been initiated into it and had added some extra movements and sound.

She had helped Robbie and Ana to find their own tone, and they found that when all three made their sounds together, they perfectly harmonised. Their sounds would blend into one until you couldn't distinguish the individual sounds anymore. Even in their own ears it sounded as one sound, as if a more whole tone was coming out of their own mouths, which was a pretty bizarre experience.

As they anchored into their own bodies, into the Earth and into Source, they became more grounded. Each connected to their as yet invisible counterpart across from them, connected to both triangles, then closed the circle.

Tiny had added some hand movements that all three were doing. It was like a modern dance as they moved in flow, their timing synced up even with their eyes closed.

Tiny spoke:

> *"Now see each colour lighting up.*
> *Start with yourself.*
> *See your own colour expanding from your heart.*
> *Now connect to the secondary colour across from you and see it expand from the heart.*
> *Now connect to the primary triangle.*
> *And now to the secondary triangle.*
> *Now close the circle.*
> *See all colours connecting into the circle.*
> *Six different rays of Light plugging into the centre,*
> *Now forming ONE BALL OF LIGHT*
> *Encoded with the Six-Crystal design."*

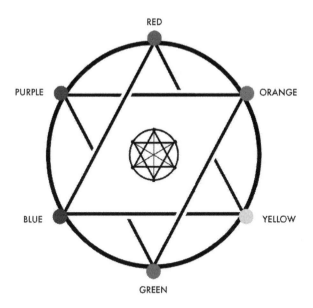

A new signal had been sent out. As always, the trio was unaware of the actual ripple it created as they opened up another level of connection with the others.

This activation had made the Six-Crystal in the hearts of the other three human beings spin. All, in their own unique life, had felt a surge of energy:

> *One was in dream state.*
> *One was under the shower.*
> *And one of them was reading a book.*

KEY CODE: COLOUR ESSENCE

59. ONE MISSION — ONE TEAM

"I had a dream last night, and there were so many different soul clusters, just all these different kinds of constellations," Tiny shared at breakfast.

"So, now I'm wondering, what if there are more Six-Crystals? Or constellations of four, or eight, or who knows, twenty? I don't know. Everything is possible, isn't it?"

"Life sure is more magical than I ever thought it could be," Robbie said.

"It sure is!" Ana chimed in. "They kept all the truth hidden in fantasy books and sacred texts. They told us it was all made up, calling it fantasy or magic, but I'm starting to believe more in magic than whatever I've learned at school." They all laughed, as they shared that feeling.

"So, what if it's true? What if there is more than one Six-Crystal?" Tiny asked quietly, which only added suspense. "Isn't it the Age of Aquarius, so our future is *destined* to be more collective? We're going back to the tribes!" Tiny had taken on some of Ana's dramatic flair from time to time. It looked good on her, and maybe a little funny as she was so, well, tiny.

"Can you imagine how much exchange there would be between different constellations?" Robbie wondered. "I mean, can you see the exponential flow of information? Haha, it just doesn't end. It goes on for infinity."

"Hell yeah!" Ana stood up from her chair. "It's like we are part of a giant mission," she said with suspense, "lightworkers from different dimensions and galaxies have decided to come to Earth at this point in time, and together give rise to the great awakening, because 'teamwork makes the dream work.'" She burst out laughing.

"But," she looked dead serious again, while looking into Tiny's eyes, "don't underestimate the tiny drop in the ocean, because together we create one big wave."

Robbie watched Tiny's and Ana's energy rising and flowing together and igniting each other's passion, creating a force field of energy that worked like a magnet for that which they spoke of and desired.

"One big team ..." Tiny dreamed away, imagining all the lightworkers spread around the world who were part of this same mission. "We can change the world together. Together we can move mountains."

Indeed, anything was possible if they would come together with a shared intention.

"I can absolutely see more constellations and clusters forming. I hold that vision for every living being, to find out who they truly are, to see why they are here on Earth, and if they choose to live by a collective design, to find their soul cluster," Robbie said.

Then immediately, he realised, "My god, it's so funny when you start to understand divine orchestration, because then you see that even your desires or hopes for others are delusional. Of course, every soul cluster is going to come together, because it's what they are designed for. So, I hope you are right, Tiny! I hope there are many more constellations, and I can't wait to see what our future will look like. But first, right here, right now, I got us some apple pie, so let's dig in, ladies. Let's get some vanilla ice cream and enjoy this very moment. Just with the three of us, as long as it lasts."

KEY CODE: ONE MISSION

3 - 6 - 9
MONTHS PASSED

(Note to reader: pick your favourite number as to what seems the most possible timeline.)

60. JUST LIKE A DREAM

Tiny had to go. She interrupted their conversation, pulled her cloak off the rack and put it on as she walked outside. Remembering there was a fair happening, she walked towards Main Street.

She was simply following an inner pull, following the inspiration without a preconceived notion of why and without a goal.

As she walked into the crowd, the music and the sounds of children playing and people laughing all faded into the background of her awareness. She paused and stood still.

He is Here.

She felt Yu-Ka-Na's presence.

With a deep inhale, she allowed her breath to slow down. Standing in the midst of the crowd, she closed her eyes. Time slowed down.

She felt him come closer.

Just like magnets drawn to each other, she felt the energy increase. Without a doubt, she recognized the signature of his energy from their many multidimensional meetings.

She opened her eyes as she turned around, and there he was.

Immediately, she saw him, amidst all the people strolling around. It seemed as if he was walking straight towards her.

Their eyes met and interlocked.

A tear fell from her cheek.

He IS Here!

His light blue skin and long, light hair had changed into a soft pale skin and short, dark chestnut hair, with eyes dark as night, but there was no doubt it was him.

Her whole body relaxed into ecstasy as a deep weight lifted from her heart.

The wholeness she had found within was immediately multiplied into another experience of Oneness now that he was here.

He stopped right in front of her while their eyes remained locked. There were no words. But they both knew.

She fell into his embrace as he held her close to his chest. With her head close to his heart, she heard his heartbeat — the proof of his aliveness in this reality.

She had found Yu-Ka-Na.

Tears of love, disbelief, magic, excitement, and overwhelm were all mixed.

After who knows how long, he softened his embrace. Taking her head between his hands, he gently kissed her on the forehead.

"I know you've been waiting for me. It took me a while to find you," he gently smiled. His deep voice sounded like liquid honey to her ears.

"Now, where are the others?"

KEY CODE: A MAGNETIC FORCE

61. NEWSFLASH

Tiny couldn't run home fast enough! She burst into the living room where Ana and Robbie were relaxing, surprised by both her sudden exit and now entrance.

"He is here!" she uttered, gasping for air. "He is here!"

"What?" Ana asked, stunned.

"I went to the fair at Main Street, and suddenly I felt his presence, like a magnet pulling me. I turned around — and he was right there! I saw him from afar and I had no doubt it was him."

Ana and Robbie listened carefully as Tiny re-enacted their meeting.

"He looked right back at me. My heart started beating faster, the world disappeared, and suddenly he stood right in front of me, staring into my eyes, and I felt like the weight of a thousand light years dropped off my shoulders."

"Did you really — meet Yu-Ka-Na?" Ana wanted to hear her confirmation, while she already knew the obvious.

Tiny approached Ana and looked into her eyes, "Tell me, am I still not dreaming?!"

Ana gently pinched her cheek as she smiled, "Nope, you're not."

"And the craziest thing — 'cause of course, there's always something crazy happening — is that he asked where the others were. Like, he *Knows*." Tiny widened her eyes to stress the fact. Indeed, Yu-Ka-Na was aware of the Six-Crystal, as his Remembrance had been activated too. It had taken him a while to find them.

"So, where is he?" Robbie asked.

"Well, he didn't want to shock you and just show up at your doorstep, so we'll meet up around 5 p.m. at the park. Oh, and by the way, his name now is Matías."

Tiny reached her hands out to Robbie and Ana, gently pulling them out of the sofa to stand up and hold hands.

"I guess our time as a triad is complete." She looked both in the eyes, one after the other.

"We are ready for the next chapter," Robbie replied.

"If this has been crazy, then I guess what's next is going to be wild," Ana remarked, and indeed, there was more to come.

KEY CODE: TOO GOOD TO BE TRUE

62. LOVE FROM VENUS

She was sitting near Lake Siskiyou, in awe of the glorious view of the mountain, while also drinking in his words. Paul of Venus, a spiritual tour guide, was talking about the mountain with deep reverence. They had gathered at the lake with a handful of other lightworkers and spiritual seekers who all had followed an inner call to visit Mount Shasta. He described the mountain as a female Being, and the way he talked about Her would forever change the way she would look at it.

With his tall wooden stick with a crystal tied to the top of it, dark glasses and a black hat that covered half his face, Paul of Venus looked like a galactic wizard who had walked right out of a fantasy movie. It was almost palpable that indeed he had descended from Venus for this incarnation here on Earth, and every word he spoke was a pure transmission, filled with exquisite codes of Love and Light that invited them all to Remember the purity of their hearts, their life's mission here on Earth, and the absolute divine nature of all of existence.

In tears, she received his words, her heart melting like butter, evoking tingles and chills across her body. Even though it was her first time visiting Mount Shasta, this place felt deeply familiar, like a sort of homecoming for her soul.

Laila had travelled all the way from England, her first crossing of the Atlantic Ocean. She had been used to the world coming to her hometown, as Glastonbury was a hot spot for mystics and spiritual pilgrims. Laila's life would read like a fairy tale to many, as she was guided by the whispers of her heart and didn't fit into any 'normal' standards of life. While other children were growing up in front of their tv, she was raised with the legends of Avalon and her mother would let her join women's circles that made ritual, magic and mysticism a normal part of her youth. By the time she was fourteen, she was getting her hands on all the books she could find about the Sisterhood of the Rose and ancient priestess lineages. As the woman she was becoming — she would soon turn twenty-one — Laila devoted her life to the wisdom of the Heart and the universal power of Love.

Paul of Venus took the group to the most powerful energy vortexes around Mount Shasta, spots she would never have found by herself. Each had a different energy signature, and at each spot, they went on a short inner journey through meditation, where Laila felt as if she was picking up different keys and frequencies to add to her backpack, in this case, her energetic field. It was more of a Remembrance than learning something new: Laila simply Remembered more of the Love she was, but in a very physical and tangible way, as if her physical body understood and reflected the message.

Paul of Venus watched Laila float around the forest. She moved gracefully, like a dancer, even when she walked. If the grass and trees could smile, they simply would, touched by her grace and elegance.

The spiritual tour ended at Headwaters Spring in Mount Shasta City Park. Laila immediately took off her sandals and tipped her toe in the fresh spring water, elated by its soft coldness. Elegantly, she jumped from one rock to another to get up close to the spring, where she filled her water bottle and cleansed her face with the water. It felt like pure crystal water coming out of the mountain, so rich, light and refreshing. She could drink this forever.

Looking into the spring, she flashed back to the day she felt the call of Mount Shasta. She had offered some roses and was sitting in prayer at Chalice Well in Glastonbury, also known as the Red Spring, when a high-pitched voice echoed in her ears, "Find the Source." The iron rails prevented her from reaching in, but her awareness was being pulled into the well to indeed 'find the Source' and follow where the water was coming from.

She allowed her awareness to travel down the well, entering deep into the Earth, following the water to where it originated from. To her surprise, it felt as if she came out on the other side of the Earth, rather than at the source of this spring, which she'd expected to find somewhere deep down in the Earth.

She wrote it off as a metaphor from her soul she hadn't been able to decipher yet, until a few days later, when she heard from a local druid that the springs in Glastonbury were connected to the spring water in Mount Shasta. That was more than 5000 miles away, in the west of the United States.

"*Holy Goddess!*" Laila thought. "*The vision showed me where to go!*" The waters had spoken to her, and she sure knew how to listen, but she couldn't have imagined meeting someone like Paul of Venus, who mirrored the possibility of being a true embodiment of Love. Maybe meeting him was the reason she was called here …

KEY CODE: WATER LINES

63. Meeting Up With Yu-Ka-Na

Ana could dance with joy as they walked to Mount Shasta City Park, eager to meet Yu-Ka-Na, or better Matías, and meet Tiny's all-time lover. She saw him from afar, sitting with Tiny, and had to giggle inside, imagining that a galactic Being had become a human man. What fantasy script had her life become? She walked towards him, squeezing Robbie's hand to calm her nerves as they drew closer.

Matías got up and first stood right in front of Robbie. The men silently looked at each other for a moment, then fell into a firm and brotherly embrace. Ana felt the bond of their camaraderie and brotherhood, even though they had just met. It moved her deeply to see two men meeting each other in such a loving, yet non-sexual way. She wasn't used to being that close with strangers, but he wasn't a stranger at all.

Before she knew it, he turned towards her with a genuine and warm smile that settled her nerves. She almost jumped into his arms to squeeze him like a teddy bear. His heartfelt hug broke the ice between them. She couldn't wait to hear him out.

"I wanna know all about you!" Ana said as soon as they all sat down on the grass.

"Haha, I can imagine you do. You don't beat around the bush, ha!" Matías responded.

"She would even love to read your mind if she could," Robbie teased, although it was not far from the truth.

"Well, I started sharing about my life with Tiny earlier, so let me give a quick summary for you now. It's not the typical story, but I'm guessing you are all pretty open-minded." Matías just double-checked before sharing more.

"We need more than some angels and alien talk to throw us off. Try us," Ana cheekily replied.

"Bueno! I'm originally from Santa Fe, but I have lived several years in Peru, near Lake Titicaca, and have spent the last two years near Mount Kailash in Tibet. These locations may seem like random facts, but one day, we can see more about their importance."

"My trip to Tibet started as a pilgrimage to the mountain known as the 'precious jewel in the snow,' but once I was there, I had nowhere else to go. It was pretty life-altering, I must say. A deep devotion sprang from within me, and I decided to stay at the monastery and live like a monk near the mountain," Matías smiled.

"After three weeks of being up the mountain, my notion of time started to disappear, the sun being the only signpost of what was day and night."

"After three months of long daily meditations, my mind had become clear, like a still lake. My Being was simply resting, and thoughts would only emerge for practical reasons, like when it was time to prepare a meal. It became clear to me how the mind can work like a precise and clear instrument."

"After six months, my body felt anew. I had lost extra weight and my body felt stronger and lighter. My body naturally healed itself, and some old aches and issues just disappeared. The chakras in my body started balancing themselves out. I became more aware of the energy flow in and around my body, and I felt like a clear conduit."

"After nine months, the veils were being lifted from my eyes. My third eye had opened and I had access to different timelines. You could call it my own past and future, but it would be more accurate to say that there are infinite parallel versions of reality and my awareness travelled to scan those most beneficial."

Matías spoke calmly, while the others hung on to his every word.

"It was around that time that this collective design started appearing in my consciousness, although it took me a while to decipher what it was about and that it was not just a metaphor or geometric form. It was a living, breathing multidimensional organism *and* there was a version of it in human form."

"And then, of course, I Remembered you, Tiny, an intergalactic love story that is playing out across so many time/space/dimensions. Wherever I Am, it seems my Being is destined to look for and find you."

Tiny's heart opened like a flower hearing Matías talk about how he had been searching for her. She felt met in one of her deepest feminine desires to be wanted.

"But how did you know she was here?" Ana asked.

"Well, first of all, it took me a few more months before I was even considering leaving the mountain, as I was mostly operating within the astral realms. I would travel in my awareness to Be with her and meet with her higher self. My consciousness would pick up information about the collective design, while all I would do was seemingly sit and meditate, yet, it feels as if my soul has travelled lifetimes in the past two years."

"But coming back to your question, Ana, it's not that I know and see everything, especially not what is actually playing out in this physical dimension. The way I found her, and found you all, is truly by following a path of breadcrumbs — a magical line-up of circumstances that unfolded, step by step. Life is one big orchestration to let this collective destiny unfold, so for those with eyes to see and ears to hear, one simply has to observe and listen to the clues that are all around us. Coincidences. Synchronicities. An intuitive hit. A desire. Many small steps taken from Tibet to being here, all the way in Shasta."

Matías looked directly at Ana. "I have found her because I could no longer *not* be with her."

His answer was still too mysterious for Ana. She still had a gazillion questions but gave up on questioning him for now. There was more time to get the ins and out of his life. Instead, she said, "I have been waiting for the day you two would meet, so I declare today as Reunion Day!"

Reunion day — it sure was!

KEY CODE: PARALLEL TIMELINES

64. AT THE PARK

The day trip with Paul of Venus had been so rich. Laila wanted to soak in all the magic, so she lay her body down in the grass in between the yellow buttercups. She felt the Earth underneath her and the sun warming her from above.

Laila was simply enjoying herself when she heard laughter in the distance, which grabbed her attention. The joy was infectious, bringing a big smile to her face. Laila turned her head and opened her eyes to see where the light-hearted sounds came from, but all she could see was the back of the two passers-by — a woman with long, curly red hair, and a man with short dark hair, wearing a brown leather jacket.

She disappeared back into her own world of bliss, until a little later, when again enticed by the sounds of laughter and cheerfulness, she rolled around on her belly to see what was happening. The couple was sitting in a circle, now accompanied by two others, and clearly enjoying themselves. They were about 80 feet away, so she couldn't hear what they were talking about, but once in a while they would burst out laughing. Laila mostly picked up the joy and giggles from the red-haired one.

She was fascinated by them, more than by the other people in the park, even though they were not the only ones. The park was filled with many beautiful souls who had come there for a walk, for meditation, playing music or just soaking up some sunshine and being replenished by the spring water.

Laila felt like she was secretly spying on them, but she was far enough away to not get caught in the act. Even though she didn't understand a word, she saw their energy field — like a giant ball of light, filled with energy waves that were exchanged between one another. Their field felt very alive, and it was not just the laughter that did it. Intrigued, she couldn't shake off her curiosity. Like a magnet, she was being pulled to join them and find out.

She stood up, grabbed her bag and sandals and confidently walked up to them. She just wanted to bathe in their energy field and feel what it was like.

"Mind if I join you?" Laila asked with bright eyes and an open smile.

Ana turned to see who had interrupted their conversation. Looking up to Laila, she felt as if she was looking at an angel as the sun highlighted her long, blonde hair with a golden balm.

"Go ahead, come and sit with us," Robbie responded as he scooted over to open the circle and make space for her.

"This can't be true," Ana whispered quietly, perplexed.

"Hi," Laila looked around the circle, "I'm Laila, by the way. Laying over there, I was so intrigued by your energy that I just had to come and feel it for myself." She said this as if it was the most normal opening sentence for a stranger. But what was normal for them these days anyway?

They each had a short exchange of names. "Hi, I'm Robbie/Ana/Matías."

"And I'm Tiny. Nice to meet you. What did our energy feel like?" she asked.

"Mmm, I saw it as one giant ball of light — with so much happening inside of it! I just couldn't resist coming over here," Laila answered. She was like an open book and wore her heart on her sleeve.

"What timing," Matías said, "you walked in on us, right on time," as if he had sight over their cosmic calendar.

"Really? What's about to happen?"

"I have no clue, but I believe you are a part of it," Ana responded, and as she looked into Laila's eyes, there was a great sense of familiarity. Her words rang true, even though Laila had no clue what was going on. Nonetheless, her heart made a little jump of excitement.

"I'm all ears. Who's gonna tell me what you're up to?" she asked the circle as she waited for someone to reveal the adventure she'd just embarked upon.

KEY CODE: ENERGY READ

65. CATCHING UP

Robbie had become a great storyteller and summarizer, so he shared the Six-Crystal design with Laila and Matías in record speed. Ana could only half listen to what he was saying as she had a brain freeze, unable to understand how both Matías and Laila had just stepped into their world out of the blue. Of course, she had been wanting this for months, yet when it happened, it literally blew her mind.

Not only was Yu-Ka-Na here in the flesh — and had Tiny found her forever lover — the Angel too had become human. It couldn't be more obvious that Laila was an Angelic Presence in human form. She was pure beauty and grace, and the love she exuded was like a constant reminder of Omnipresent Love. Ana couldn't look at her too much, as it made her tear up. She was still adjusting to sitting next to her and feeling her energy beaming like a lighthouse. The Six-Crystal had definitely become more alive in just one afternoon.

Meanwhile, Tiny too was in a kind of trance, as all she could feel and think of was her reunion with Matías. It felt as if they were continuously talking to each other without words, and she could read his feelings and responses even before he uttered a word. She too had just entered a whole new reality, even though the Earth was still spinning and the clock still ticking.

"And so, you believe that I am a part of this Six-Crystal?" Laila commented, after receiving Robbie's summary. "I have never heard of this design before, but it doesn't even sound like a surprise. My body received your words with utter peace and in full resonance. I Know how the Goddess speaks to me and I know how to listen. That's what brought me here, and now I'm sitting here in your circle."

Her reason for being there was revealing itself by the minute.

"So, this is my soul family," Laila looked full of wonder at each of them, "or soul cluster, as you call it, Robbie." She could feel each one's energy, complementary to hers, each contributing a unique piece to the whole.

"There is only one thing I want to do then," Laila shared, "I want to see what this Six-Crystal is about. I want to see what the Goddess has in store for us."

Laila's appearance had indeed opened up a new level of seeing and foreseeing what was possible now. It was time for another future glimpse of what the Six-Crystal could become.

KEY CODE: SYNCING UP

66. THE HIGHEST POTENTIAL

Peeking into the future would always be limited by their current perspective of what they believed to be true and possible. Yet together, they would be able to see more of the highest potential as their individual limitations would be balanced out by the whole.

Ana, Tiny and Laila lay on their backs in the grass, while Robbie and Matías sat cross-legged in a meditation pose. They had opened up the circle as if SiX sat among them as well, imagining SiX being there with them energetically. As it was the first time the five of them were together physically, the energy was definitely amplified, to the point where the young women had to lie down to let the energy course through their bodies.

Tiny started by guiding them through the Activation Ritual so each would be anchored within themselves, as well as locked into their position within the Six-Crystal. Next, Robbie invited them to connect to their formless nature and let go of all they knew about themselves and life, as if they instead would be swimming in an infinite field of pure potential. In this empty, yet alive space, they could call in the highest potential of the Six-Crystal to reveal itself. Each, in their own way, tuned in to this potential, and each received a piece of the puzzle that showed a glimpse of that actual reality.

Ana's Seeing:

We are all together, sitting in a circle.

Each one looks like a strong, solid, unshakeable pillar.
Six pillars of Light, together forming one big field of Light.

It's as if the whole space is lighting up,
highlighted by white sunlight,
without there being a sun.

I recognize each one of us,
yet our physical forms look blurred,
faded by the white Light.

It's harder to see the differences between us
and easier to see that, indeed,
We are One
and the same.

Would there be any other way of describing this field,
than to call it a Giant Field of Light and Love?

Ana's body and mind couldn't even grasp the subtleties and richness of this collective field, but she could feel how it elevated her spirit. She didn't see many more details, as her awareness faded and merged with the field itself. She was simply basking in its light, while energetically receiving the full imprint of its highest potential.

Robbie also imagined them sitting in a circle as the next piece revealed itself to him.

Robbie's Seeing:

As we sit in a circle,
someone else walks into the centre,
standing right in the middle
with closed eyes.

The energy of our collective field
is directed into the midpoint,
as if all the energy from our hearts
is beaming and being pointed to the middle.

I see the person explode,
shattering into pieces,
although it looks more like the snake shedding its skin.

What is being dropped are his masks,
the costume of his personality he was wearing,
the expectations of others he had taken on.
What's false fades away, and what is left is nothing but
what's true.

What emerges from within
is the same person
in pure Light.
Free,
extending his arms wide open,
head tilted back,
opening up his lungs and chest as if he can finally breathe.

A giant energy release.
Golden Light swirling around his body
and spiralling upwards.

He too now Remembers.
He has become Him-Self.
He Knows who he is,
without a doubt.

Our collective field works like a healing balm.
Revealing Truth where limitation was held.

Robbie was in touch with the transformative and awakening capacity of their field. They no longer had to take on a role of being a healer or teacher. Their field worked its magic. Simply approximating it started to have a ripple effect on others. Their collective field was also a most powerful vehicle for manifestation and creation.

Anything that is wanted and desired,
and held within the core of the Six-Crystal,
is destined to become reality.

Anything that is honouring free will,
taking the whole into account
and including the Highest Good of All,
will be yours.

Robbie didn't need more specifics. He understood the reach of what they were capable of. They could move mountains if they wanted to, or build another pyramid. The choice was theirs, although he was pretty sure more details would reveal themselves, in divine timing, of course.

Tiny and Matías were viewing simultaneously and received similar visions, just from different angles.

"Dreaming Heaven on Earth into reality,
that's what we are here for," Tiny thought.

"A desire held for every human being
so it would be a lived experience," Matías shared in response.

They could see it required a shift in consciousness, a Remembrance, and the ability to be in harmony with All of Life.

Heaven on Earth
does not have a specific or single form.
It is up to All to play and to create,
and to envision and bring their glorious visions into existence.

Their collective desire was to simply pave a pathway for all of humanity to enter this Golden Age where Heaven on Earth is lived and embodied.

Remembering One-Self
and syncing up with the whole
as we move and live as One.

Tiny wanted to see more of what Heaven on Earth would look like for their Six-Crystal, and her curiosity allowed for more information to be seen.

I Am Home.
Surrounded by lush, green nature,
the mountains and big rocks giving grounding,
while the waterfalls and ocean waves allow us to flow.

Streaming water
connects the different parts
of our living village.

The whole area feels like one living, breathing organism.
Thriving, alive, energised.
There is continuous expansion,
where all life forms grow in perfect harmony.

Matías zoomed in again on the future of their soul cluster.

Step by step,
we have been tapping into forgotten abilities
as new sequences in our DNA unlocked.

It's pure play to explore.

Telepathy has been established between us.
Words are used with precision and honour.
Chit chat is replaced by songs and poetry,
and All of Life feels like poetry in motion,

*transmitting different frequencies,
all encoded with pure joy, ease and play.*

*We are even playing with gravity.
I can't levitate yet by myself,
but as a whole, within our field,
we are experimenting and playing with lifting someone up
in the centre of the circle,
as well as moving objects around.
We burst into celebration whenever we succeed.*

*There is not one hair on our head
that would think of using or misusing these abilities
to gain power and self-gain.
It is pure play,
the expansion and joy of creation,
and an absolute delight
to be experiencing more infinite potential in form.*

*The ladies are playing around with adjusting their
physical forms.
Changing eye colour, erasing some wrinkles,
adjusting their body to have a more timeless form and
stop aging,
purely by will.*

Matías, too, realised there was no end to their abilities and anchored deeper into Remembering his own unlimited nature.

Laila was enthralled by the question 'what is this Six-Crystal about?' and didn't just get information about how they would operate together, but even more so, how they were only preparing the grounds.

> *The Six-Crystal is like a portal.*
>
> *A group of souls is wanting to come through and enter this field.*

Laila could see a group of souls that wanted to be born in their collective field. It was probably the next iteration of a soul cluster, but this time around, these souls wanted to come in together and with full Remembrance.

> *The Veil of Forgetfulness is no longer needed when the Six-Crystal is in full effect.*
>
> *Our coming together*
> *is part of a diligent preparation*
> *to create a whole new environment*
> *for souls to enter into.*

Laila could see how the harshness of life on Earth, with its old ways of power, greed, corruption, disconnect and separation would be too harsh to bear. These highly sensitive souls wanted to come into a collective field of Harmony, Oneness and Love.

> *These souls are not birthed in traditional family systems.*
> *They are meant to be raised in 'come-unity.'*

The Six-Crystal was designed to become the birthing vessel for a group of souls, of children, who wanted to come to Earth soon, and who each carried higher frequencies and codes that had not yet been anchored onto Earth. They literally would carry so much Light encoded in their Being, that growing up in a united field was a prerequisite for them even being able to exist in a physical, human form.

Laila flashed forward into the future.

She could see how the Six-Crystal, at the level of their higher self as a united consciousness, was now negotiating with this next generation soul cluster, exploring the possibilities of redesigning birth and changing the contracts for entering Earth.

What if a woman no longer had to carry a baby for nine months?

They discussed the option of immaculate conception, but kept getting hints, seeing that these souls would quite literally just 'drop' into their field and materialise 'out of thin air.'

It defied all logic, but by now, they had seen and experienced so much that they were actively exploring the magical and impossible realms, knowing that all that can be imagined can become a reality. It was just a matter of checking what would be most relevant for these souls and seeing if they still needed a physical gestation period of growth and evolution in a female's womb.

And just like birth, death was also being renegotiated and simplified. When the fear of death disappears, a lot of suffering and deterioration can be prevented.

To the Six-Crystal, it was pretty simple. When one lives in alignment with their soul and higher self, it becomes crystal clear what one's life purpose and mission is, and when it has been completed.

One can then still, through free will, decide if there are any other experiences to be had or lessons to be learned, if there is more that can be added to creation. But ultimately, one can discern and know when the time has come to pass on to the next phase and complete their life on Earth.

Instead of a slow or painful death, one could simply choose to leave this physical human suit. Then, the heart would stop beating and the spirit would leave the body/mind vehicle and go into the next phase of its evolution of reviewing its life journey.

Laila had read a lot of mystical books and was familiar with the godlike abilities men had in ancient times, but this information was pretty jaw-dropping, especially as it concerned her own future.

Each, in their own timing, completed their future glimpse and needed some time to adjust and bring their awareness back to their current experience. The future glimpse became like a memory already lived within their awareness, which would naturally propel them towards it.

After some time in silence, each shared their download, and each listened with full presence to what was being exchanged. They all tapped into the same future potential of what was possible for them as a Six-Crystal.

"I'm having chills," Ana shivered. "Do you guys actually think this is and can be real?"

Robbie gazed around and felt the solidness in the others. "Anyone who doesn't believe this is real?" he asked.

"It's not a matter of believing it is real or not," Laila answered. "To the mind, this may always seem surreal. From our current viewpoint, we will never be able to fully grasp if and how this can happen. What matters is if it feels true, if it resonates in our heart so that it pierces through all the mind chatter and just feels like a full body 'Yes!'" Her words naturally brought lightness to the topic. "And I sense we are all feeling the truth of this."

They all looked at each other as if they had just said yes and had committed to each other to be on this quest.

Truth was, it didn't matter how much or how little their minds resisted, as there was such a strong magnetic force field between the five of them that was continuously gearing up towards more unity, more harmony and more resonance.

"Now we are just waiting for SiX to come join us," Tiny said with a smile.

"Or SiX is waiting for us to find him or her," Matías posed the alternative.

"Let's start with getting to know each other more," Robbie proposed. "I know it's a bit weird, as I feel like I know the depths of your Being, but I hardly know anything about you or your human lives so far."

"Or if you like coffee, tea or a green matcha," Ana added, like a real barista.

"And what now? Is everyone here willing to give up their old life, to be together, and move together, and do life together?" Tiny asked. It was almost a rhetorical question, but it was good for each to consciously make the choice to say yes to their adventuring as a Six-Crystal.

"I feel like I have travelled dimensions to come and find you, Tiny, and to reunite again with all of you, this time in physical form, so I ain't got nowhere else to go," Matías responded, both dead serious and light-hearted.

"Same for me," Robbie replied.

"I didn't know what I would find by coming here to Mount Shasta," Laila giggled, "but I sure didn't expect to find my soul family. There's nowhere else I'd rather be. It's obvious we signed up for this adventure long ago!" Her eagerness flowed out from her words.

"Do I even have a choice?" Ana asked with some irony. "I still don't know what I'm getting myself into, and the uncertainty of it still scares me in moments, like I'm losing my grip of everything I have ever known, but I can't ignore this pull within me. I literally feel like I don't have another choice but to say yes to this." She felt their eyes piercing through her.

"And yes, yes, of course, I do *want* this! I have made my choice. I'm not a victim here to my own destiny. I'm all in, with all I got." Robbie pulled Ana up close and kissed her on the head, acknowledging her brave heart.

"You know this all sounds like a 'too good to be true' movie at times, right? Like, I have to keep pinching myself." Touched by their answers, Tiny simultaneously sighed and laughed.

"Let's meet here again tomorrow for our next adventure," Ana proposed.

"Yes, and let's go to the waterfalls nearby," Robbie suggested. "I bet you haven't seen them yet, Laila, and I'm sure you'll love it. It's like a mystical fairyland, with the Earth brimming with liveliness and the water like liquid crystals that recharge your body."

"Sounds like a divine plan!" Laila responded with enthusiasm.

"To be continued!" Ana concluded. "See y'all tomorrow!"

Laila decided to stay a little longer at the park and lay in the grass while the sun kissed her skin.

Robbie and Ana walked back home, while Tiny and Matías went out to have dinner, almost like it was their first date night.

And SiX?

SiX just finished the final chapter of the Book he/she/they were reading.

Would SiX finally realise the divine orchestration that had played out to make him/her/them wake up to their own collective nature?

You better tell me ...

YOU ARE THE KEY CODE

THE SIX-CRYSTAL SPEAKS

I AM THE SIX-CRYSTAL
An impeccable multidimensional design,
spinning and swirling
in a dimension without time and space.

I AM THE SIX-CRYSTAL
Six points
spinning in complete harmony,
tethered in a unique constellation,
exploring different pathways towards the same goal.

I AM THE SIX-CRYSTAL
All information is already stored within me.
All possible outcomes, timelines and potentials already held,
infinite possibilities happening simultaneously.

I AM THE SIX-CRYSTAL

Everything birthed from this design
has the Six-Crystal embedded at its core.
You can know me through the whole,
or through each of the separate parts.

Even if you can identify six different aspects,
simultaneously they are One,
inseparable, interconnected and indivisible.

I AM THE SIX-CRYSTAL

We appear as a collective consciousness.
And so, the 'I Am' equals the 'We are'.
As the Six-Crystal, We are One and Move as One.

It is our desire to experience our Oneness
in all forms and all ways.
Therefore, we contemplate the path of splitting
our collective nature back into individual threads,
that each can find their way back home,
towards the Oneness they once seemingly left,
yet simultaneously stem from,
and therefore, can never be fully away from.

We bend ourselves into different time, space
and dimensional structures,
existing at each level of reality as different expressions
to explore how this design moves across different octaves,
and how Oneness, or the seeming separation from it,

can be experienced in infinite ways.
The Veil of Forgetfulness that appears in 3D on Earth,
and the illusion of separation,
can only sustain itself for a limited time
- that is in Earth years -
before the magnetic force field of the Six-Crystal itself
pulls all aspects back into their constellation,
into their original design,
to be whole again as One.

When these six aspects
reunite and come together,
they enter a different realm of possibility
and form a new harmonic,
able to create a new octave of experiences.

By breaking the spell of separation,
they can now step into their co-creator mode,
as Divine Creators of the reality they shape around them.

This is not a becoming,
but a Remembrance of what has always been.

It does not matter what is created
through the Six-Crystal in its human formation.

What matters is the Remembrance
of being whole and moving as One.
What matters is the experience and embodiment
of unity consciousness in 3D form.

This is the design.
This is the desire.
This is the intention.

As the story unfolds, the design unravels itself and gets to be lived.

BLURRED LINES

Dear Reader,

I have come a long way to enter the portal of your heart, beyond the limitations of your mind. I Am right Here by your side, even though you may not see or feel me. I know it is quite miraculous how this Book has appeared in your hands, or in front of your eyes.

Even though it may appear that I Am the One who has written this Book, I hope this letter helps you realise that it is you who has called this into creation.

This Book is a living example of divine orchestration by our higher selves, who came up with the inspiration of bringing this Book into form so it could become a great accelerator for you to Awaken, Remember and Activate your purpose and your own collective design.

Yes — you are SiX.

The one missing piece in the whole.

You are the One we have been waiting for.
You are the One who makes the whole complete.
You are as unique as a snowflake and truly irreplaceable,
as there is no-One like you.

You are Here for a reason.

Your purpose wants to be lived, and your contribution will not only be life-changing, but world-changing.

Superiority or grandiosity are not required to live that, rather, a humility to devote yourself to the actual greatness of the Divine that wants to flow through you.

And yes, you are part of a greater
and more collective design.
The future is collective.

It's the Age of Aquarius after all in case you need some external validation to believe it's true.

You cannot stop this from happening.

You can try and slow it down, resist it, and even deny it — OR — you can allow the flow to take you and all you've known, rewriting the scripts of your life and what reality looks like, opening up new possibilities of what appears to be magical, which is actually just you unlocking your multidimensionality in your human form.

I Know you Remember.
I Know you have glimpsed it.
I Know you have felt it.
I Know you Know ... deep down.

AND

I also Know you have doubts.
You don't fully Trust yourself and your seeing.
You fear what is possible and how many changes will occur in your life, afraid of what will be left of what you've known and cherished.
You desire to live your highest potential with all your heart, yet the comforts of your life want you to hold on to what has been.

It's simply a choice, dear One. What more do you need to get confirmation that there is more to you and this life?

Isn't your higher self communicating through a book that ended up in your hands enough of a miraculous twist to make you believe in the extraordinary?

What more magic and miracles do you need as a permission slip to believe that you are not meant to live life according to the rules you have learned?

These rules were never meant to be your cage and you Know it, for they limit your true nature.

When will you treat this lifetime as the precious gem it is?

When will you stop wasting time, oblivious to the fact that you have no clue when your time here will come to an end?

When will you step into the role of the hero in the movie of your life and decide that you are the courageous, magnificent, unlimited One you have been waiting for?

When will you be the co-creator of what you call your reality?

Now, shall we change up the future tense to the present tense?

> *Can you …*
> *Will you …*
> *Do you SAY YES to your own unique, greater design RIGHT NOW?*
> *Without a clue as to what and how that will look like — it does not matter, yet.*

It starts with this very moment, this one moment in time, where you get to make a declaration to the whole universe and send out a signal that ripples out across space and time — and yes, you can be sure that you are being witnessed by All of Life as you do.

A holy YES, which bursts out from your heart, like an offering of your life into the hands of your soul and a surrender to your Higher Self.

> *It's just one simple word.*
> *But allow it to be the turning point of your lifetime,*
> *because that is what this Book is intended to be,*
> *a turning point in your life.*
> *There was a before, and there will be an after.*

> *So let me ask this question one more time: Are You saying YES to the greater design of your life?*
> *Insert your answer here:……………………………………………*
> *Note: your answer has already been recorded in the Akashic Records.*

We both already knew what the answer would be, so there is no surprise.

And yes, your mind is boggled — how is it possible that this Book is written to you, and to every other reader, at the same time? Oh yes, it is possible, as this Book is a multidimensional vehicle. As a skeleton key that fits every door, so does this Book act like a key, unlocking different aspects in every reader.

Let this be just the beginning of seeing how life works in mysterious, miraculous and multidimensional ways. The best is yet to come, dear One!

And don't forget to take to heart the invitation that awaits you in the following pages, expanding this experience from a one-directional stream between you and me into a multi-directional stream with other readers and, who knows, your soul family.

Our hearts rejoice in the Remembrance that is, has been and will be activated through the Six-Crystal coming back into your life. That it may continue to unravel itself for you in the most beneficial of ways, for the Highest Good of All.

With Love, and endless Devotion,

I Am Cleo
Writer of the Book

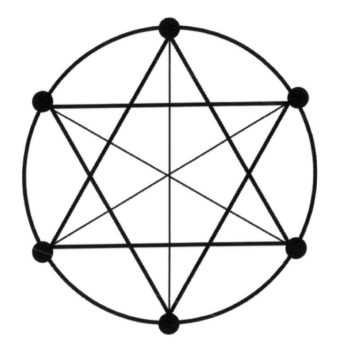

Now let the Six-Crystal live within you …

MY INVITATION TO YOU

You are invited to join **The Six-Crystal Book Ques**t, a multidimensional adventure where readers from around the globe meet and exchange insights about this book.

Imagine …

* receiving new insights about the Key Codes within the Six-Crystal manuscript. *#newdownloadsincoming*
* finding greater confidence, clarity and courage in relation to your soul's mission. *#activation*
* being part of a unique group of souls who embark on this online quest together and get a glimpse of what unity is like. *#divinemeetings*

Yes, imagine being part of a book club that doesn't just enrich your reading experience but profoundly impacts your life, in the most unexpected ways.

This book is simply a doorway to a whole new world that is wanting to open up to you.

If this book evoked Remembrance and recognition in you, and was like a *#homecoming*, then you are more than welcome to join us on this quest.

✶ HERE IS MY GIFT TO YOU ✶

The Six-Crystal Book Quest
FREE TICKET

Find out when the next quest starts & how to sign up:
www.thesixcrystal.com

What other readers say:

"The Quest elevated the book experience to a whole new level. Sharing insights & aha-moments with a group led to discovering how magically interwoven our life experiences are." —*Diane*

"This Book Quest was like a Homecoming. A confirmation that I'm not alone in my visions of Heaven on Earth. What a gift to meet these souls by whom I felt seen & supported." —*Hilde*

I would love to bridge our worlds and meet you on this Quest!

With Soul,
Stephanie Claus

POSSIBLE NEXT STEPS

WHY DID YOU COME TO EARTH?

A guided audio journey I created for you to get in touch with your soul's intention and desire for coming to Earth at this point in time.

Access the FREE audio here: **www.thesixcrystal.com/audio**

THE SIX-CRYSTAL - ORACLE CARDS

Let the Key Codes of this book become a messenger in your daily life and use them for divination, inspiration and guidance, with breathtaking artwork by Charlie Orellana (www.aephicles.com).

Discover the oracle deck here: **www.thesixcrystal.com/oraclecards**

THE FINAL CHANCE PODCAST

What if you only have sixty minutes left to share your message, truth and legacy with the world? That is the main question in the Final Chance podcast, featuring inspiring conversations with purpose-driven, passionate changemakers and multidimensional Beings who let you into their hearts and world. Beautiful transmissions with people who impacted my own life's journey!

Season 1 is available on Spotify & YouTube, or go to:
www.thesixcrystal.com/podcast

THE SIX-CRYSTAL

Go to the main website of the Six-Crystal to discover the latest news, offerings & updates.

Go to **www.thesixcrystal.com**

RECOMMENDED RESOURCES

With great Love, I have selected a few resources and Beings that have played a part in my own journey of Remembrance — that they may inspire you too.

PILAR LESKO

All things 'Energy Mastery' and 'Frequency First' life and business. Tune into her website to find her latest offerings:
www.pilarlesko.com

PAUL OF VENUS

Explore Mount Shasta through his eyes and your world will be changed.
You can book a private tour, be part of a group tour or join a retreat:
https://mtshastaspiritualtours.com

VERONIKA RENIERS

For Dutch readers, I invite you to go check out her creations. Her book *'Merlijn en het sluiten van de poorten'* has been my all-time favourite and is another multidimensional book that evokes a deep Remembrance:
https://www.elfling.be/hetoudevolk

THE STARSEED ORACLE

This oracle deck has offered a lot of guidance and confirmation during my writer's journey and is a very soul-nourishing deck for starseeds and lightworkers.
You can order The Starseed Oracle by Rebecca Campbell online:
https://starseedoracle.me/

JEWELS OF SILENCE BY ASHANA

This music album played endlessly on repeat while I was writing and editing this book. I highly recommend you read this book while listening to her Crystal Singing.
You can find the album *Jewels of Silence* on Spotify.

SOUL PHOTOGRAPHY

Landa Penders is the beautiful creatrix of the picture on the back cover of this book. She knows how to capture your Essence in a light and playful way:
www.landapenders.com

AEPHICLES - MULTIDIMENSIONAL DIGITAL ART

Charlie Orellana is the creator of the cover art of this book, as well as the designs for the oracle cards. Pure synchronicity — and social media — led me to work with this amazing artist to translate the key codes of this book into captivating visuals. Consider working with him for your own oracle deck, music album art, festival posters, whatever your soul calls you to create.

www.aephicles.com

SYMBOLS & ART

Anje Hoff created the symbols of the Six-Crystal activation and thus added her magic touch to this creation. She is a young artist who is following her own quest and travelling as a nomad through Europe, but I know, one day the world will get to see, hear and read more about her creations.

www.anjehoff.nl

KATALPA LIFE CENTER

The Katalpa field holds a frequency of inner peace, stillness and purity, and offers a transformational space as soon as you enter through the gate. Katalpa is where you get to experience what it means to become deeply still, connect to your heart and soul, and sync up with that greater flow of life that moves us all. Feel welcome to stay at Katalpa Life Center in Belgium.

www.katalpalifecenter.be

THE INSPIRED WRITER PROGRAM

Do you feel like there's a book inside of you and you've been postponing writing or don't know where to start? Allow Rachael Jayne & Datta Groover to connect you to the Soul of your book and guide you to write in pure Divine Flow. See all offered programs at: **https://theawakenedschool.com** and check out 'The Inspired Writer.'

MASSARO UNIVERSITY

Connect. Learn. Awaken.

A learning and community platform for the spiritual seeker, the aspiring pure leader and the sincere student of Life Itself.

MU is school as school was meant to be: an ongoing charging station that nurtures your connection to Source (Self-Realization), gives you the tools and consistent support to awaken and ascend yourself, and helps you optimize your manifestations of your Self into this world (Self-Actualization), for the benefit of all.

If you want to know yourself, and desire to be of service to the ignition of global awakening, Massaro University offers ongoing and ever-expanding learning opportunities to support your soul's evolution in an inspiring and dedicated community environment.

Go to: **www.Massaro.University**

GRATITUDE

I BOW TO THE SOUL OF THIS BOOK

I am filled with deep gratitude for being chosen to bring you into form. Your Essence feels like mine, and yet your wisdom and guidance has not stopped inspiring and guiding me.

I SING A SONG OF GRATITUDE TO ALL MY BOOK ANGELS

You each have offered your time, energy and Love to this book, supported me through moments of doubt and hesitation, and you made the magic of this book come alive and showed me it was real — not just for me.

Thank you, Diane, for your clear eye, catching my mistakes as a non-native English speaker. Thanks to you there are no longer 'whales' lost in the story.

Thank you, Maia, for your presence and receptivity while I read the book out loud for the very first time. Luckily, we combined hours of reading with some good food, and I appreciate our time together.

Thank you, Erika, for believing in me and my message.

Thank you, Els, for receiving this book energetically and beyond.

Thank you, Bart and Janneke, for being my mini-audience and allowing this book to become more alive through our sharings and lives.

Thank you, dear Book Encoders — Itotia, Karissa, Elanteh, Naduah

& Sahira — for weaving a multidimensional tapestry between this manuscript and the readers.

Thank you to all future Book Ambassadors, for creating new possibilities and opportunities and allowing this book to spread its wings and fly.

A LITTLE EXTRA LOVE TO MY SOUL ALLIES

Especially to Karissa and Sahira, for playing with me in the infinite field of possibilities, always choosing expansion, and Remembering our connection across dimensions. Thank you for blessing me with your grace, beauty, and all-embracing Love.

DEEP GRATITUDE IN MY HEART FOR RACHAEL JAYNE & DATTA GROOVER

This book would not have been here without your free book challenge, the Inspired Writer Retreat and Deep Pacific Press Published Author Program. You have created a seamless birthing canal to help these soulful books come into form, and help writers overcome procrastination, doubt and hesitation. You have helped me become a writer and author — in a very graceful way. To take me step by step from writing, through editing, and all the way to publishing — what a gift!

Thanks to the whole team of Deep Pacific Press for your expertise along the way, especially to Jennifer Snowball, for answering my every question and request.

Thank you Karen Collyer, for upgrading this manuscript and making it more readable through your editing skills.

SPECIAL THANKS

To the White Wolf, for diligently being by my side while writing.

To Cleo, my Highest Self, for anchoring me into a more expanded version of myself.

Thanks to Stephen from Gurushasta for offering a beautiful haven, where I downloaded the first draft of this book in a most magical setting.

Thanks to Truus Druyts for helping me uncover some of my deepest wounds that held me back from sharing my voice and message.

Thanks to Charlie Orellana for letting the key codes come to life in visual masterpieces, to Anje Hoff for creating the symbols, and to Landa Penders for capturing my Essence and beauty on camera.

And of course, thank you to my family, for offering me the greatest playground to learn about Love in this incarnation. Mama, Jaak & Xander, I'm deeply grateful for all the love and care I received while my body was healing.

A SPECIAL SHOUT-OUT TO MY ANGEL INVESTOR

My Angel Investor, you made the creation of the oracle cards possible in service to the Highest Good of All, reminding me that our divine creations are always supported. That your gift may be one that keeps on giving.

THANK YOU TO EVERY READER

Because believe it or not, I have felt you every step along the way. It's as if you all gathered around me in a circle while I was writing, and I have felt extremely supported. You have reminded me that this book is needed, and that You wanted this.

Thank you to All who expressed their curiosity and desire to read this book before it was published. Thank you for this special co-creation!

THANK YOU TO THE SIX-CRYSTAL AND MY SOUL TRIBE

You have been a part of me for more than five years now and have shown me a future glimpse I can't shake off.

I Know why I Am Here, and I Know I will live this collective imprint before I die. The best is truly yet to come.

If you are in Love with this book,
if you have felt its activations and gained new insights,
or if it is leading you to a turning point in your life …

Remember,

SHARING IS CARING

Feel free to share this book
with other starseeds and lightworkers.

Why not get a copy as a birthday gift to someone,
or recommend it to your friends and community.

Share about the Six-Crystal on social media and tag:
Instagram: @claus.stephanie
@thesixcrystal

If you want to book Stephanie Claus as a speaker for your event,
or as a podcast guest, email:
connect@stephanieclaus.com

And of course, LOVE to see you soon in the Book Quest!
Discover more:
www.thesixcrystal.com

Made in the USA
Monee, IL
16 September 2024